OUR CHILDREN
AND
OURSELVES

by

ETIENNE DE GREEFF

TRANSLATED BY
THE EARL OF WICKLOW

WITH AN INTRODUCTION BY
REV. E. F. O'DOHERTY, M.A., D.PH.
Professor of Logic and Psychology, University College, Dublin

alba house
A DIVISION OF ST. PAUL PUBLICATIONS
Staten Island, New York 10314

NIHIL OBSTAT

IOANNES O'DONOGHUE
CENSOR. THEOL. DEPUT.

IMPRIMI POTEST

✠ IOANNES CAROLUS,

ARCHIEP. DUBLINEN., HIBERNIAE PRIMAS.

VII JAN. MCMLVIII.

*Alba House is staffed by the Pauline Priests and Brothers
Society of St. Paul, Staten Island, N.Y.* 10314

MADE AND PRINTED IN THE REPUBLIC OF IRELAND

Contents

Contents

Preface

Although the volume of literature about childhood and adolescence is immense, and a great deal of it is valuable, it is only too true that not all of it is reliable. Many works which might be helpful are vitiated by lack of ethical principles, or by their complete ignoring of the rational and spiritual, or by a tacit or explicit repudiation of Christian teaching. Some of the popular works on these topics which fall into the hands of parents tend to shake the parents' confidence in their own powers to rear their children properly. Some again, owing to an exaggerated respect for the science of education, lay down as principles or norms propositions which are neither established as true nor even accepted by other equally expert educationists. Dr. de Greeff is very much alive to all this. He rightly deplores the exaggerated claims of some educational and psychological experts. There are few greater evils in the intellectual world than false psychology and faulty pedagogy.

It is not surprising therefore that sane and trustworthy books on childhood and adolescence are rare. Rarer still are readable works which can be recommended to parents as a help towards understanding their own children. We must therefore be grateful to Lord Wicklow and the publishers for making available in an English translation the work *Nos Enfants et Nous* by Dr. de Greeff. Writing in a pungent, trenchant and often difficult style, Dr. de Greeff unravels some of the mysteries and reveals some of the beauty of human personality through childhood and adolescence. Deep psychological insight, the product of intellect tempered by profound but controlled emotion, make this an exciting work. The author's deep faith and great charity, added to his professional skill as a psychologist, make Dr. de Greeff almost unique among authors on these topics. Though occasionally impassioned, his writing is never polemical. Dr. de Greeff defends the family as a necessary and natural institution, not only on philosophical and theological grounds, but also on the basis of the empirical evidence as psychology reveals it in the personality of the child. Many recent investigations of children and adolescents support the age-old principles of Catholic doctrine concerning the nature and status of the family, the obligations and duties of parents and children, the role of family life in education: so much so indeed, that from the point of view of the welfare of the child it is almost true to say that even a bad family is better than a good institution.

Those who are professionally interested in children, to whom the mystery of a child's mind is alternately fascinating and bewildering, will gain much from reading this work.

E. F. O'DOHERTY.

CHAPTER ONE

The Call to Life

I

A short time ago, in the course of a lecture dealing with eugenics, I heard the lecturer affirm vehemently, as if he were saying the last word on the subject, that in natural morality that which did not yet exist had not the right to do so, and had no claim to influence the behaviour of a man. In the thought of the lecturer, that which did not exist was the possible child, the descendant of a couple. And if I understood the theologian correctly, the conclusions he had reached were more or less as follows: "Do not worry about the future and above all, since the future does not yet exist, do not let it make any claims on you, just do your duty and trust in Providence."

It is possible that, in the mechanical order, that which does not yet exist has no rights. But I do not know if this religious man of science, in stating the precept which I have just quoted, was aware of the full meaning of his words; if he understood that his argument, from the purely human point of view, by denying all rights to the possible child, entailed such a serious refusal to take into account the full scope of his acts, that no normal, honest man who was conscious of what he was doing, could possibly accept it. Paternity does not usually come till an age has been reached when the future with its uncertainties is pictured as forming part of the present. The normal adult man regards the present with a glance that at the same time looks several years ahead, and that is why such a man is not a weakling and is no longer a child. To ask him to be partially indifferent to the possible consequences of actions which he performs today, is to ask him to take up an attitude that is contrary to nature. If I have not enough dialectical skill to bring this curious argument to nothing, I can anyway affirm one thing: men who are really indifferent to the future are only to be found in prisons, and there are not many of them.

Such indifference, which is not normally to be found among men, is even less likely to be found amid the paternal instincts. A well brought up man, whose moral sense has developed in such a way that the full flowering of his personality can be achieved, meets, at a certain moment

9

of his existence, with an uneasy desire for progeny. He rarely recognizes that in this intimate experience the profound appeal of an instinct is at work, but precisely because he fails to recognize the instinct, and because the latter acts by influencing the intellectual and affective dispositions which he already possesses, there is no sphere in which a mature man, conscious of the significance of his acts, is less able to escape from the pang of responsibility, where life is concerned. This sense of uneasiness, which represents a great motive power, should not be eliminated, but trained and directed towards a definite end.

We are not here discussing a principle: from this stage onwards only a man of an uneducated and retrograde mentality would submit blindly to the facile theory that it is the duty of Providence to make up for his own carelessness. No man who has learnt the limits within which he can influence the course of the future, and that in the domain which he holds dearest, is capable of not taking this into account.

Instead of wasting our time in idle discussions as to the rights or the lack of rights of the child which does not yet exist, we would hold it to be a determined fact that there is an absolute continuity between the parents and the child, a continuity which is evident not only from the organic point of view, but is also evident in the moral personalities of the parents, and this continuity has certain consequences long before the child is there.

The first of these consequences is naturally the desire to behave as worthily as possible in this order of things, and to learn about all that concerns it.

II

It would certainly seem to be no small error to identify the problem of education with the question of the moral or social type to which it is hoped the child will conform later on. This problem is certainly of the highest importance and must always be kept in view. But we must not forget that the moral and social type of man whom we wish to form, and will up to a point succeed in doing, will *never be more than its outward appearance:* the true values of a man are not to be found in those qualities through which we see him, but in the more or less profound harmony between his inner personality, which is known by nobody and least of all by himself, a profound personality which certainly represents the true result of his education, and his external personality, which is partially made by himself but is dominated by the tendency to imitate and to conform with his surroundings. This means that we are able to say: whatever the type may appear to be which we wish to produce, there is a preliminary formation of the personality, a formation which is independent of all religious and racial considerations, tending to create certain intellectual and affective reactions in the child, ways of behaviour and compensation which are on the one hand in conformity with his constitution and his temperament, and on the other hand with the general situation that life presents. This means that if we hold that the great end of education should be to teach how to love and to serve, that the object of this love should be God, or country, or race, or humanity, then it is of the first importance that the child should learn how to love, and to love in a certain way.

Having admitted this, we shall then see that good intentions are not enough, that to succeed in education more is needed than the imposition of a formula of life which holds good everywhere. Real education will avoid the use of definitive formulas, and will turn its attention to the obscure domain of the unconscious and its automatic movements; these together form the deep personality, which is at all times *independent* and master of these appearances of which it makes use, by processes of adaptation and deformation which are unexpectedly complicated, so that under cover of them it may realise its blind destiny.

III

If we take into account the difficulty of the end to be attained, if for one instant we were to admit the hypothesis that education should be a work which at every point is consciously thought out, we should draw back, startled at the complexity of the work and the poverty of the knowledge and means at our disposal. I know well that teachers imagine an era of learning is on the way and think there is a time soon ahead when every mother will model herself on Mme. Montessori. But I know that, in spite of the teachers, the normal well-balanced mother will always remain a real mother; our aim must be not to replace the mother by an educator, but solely to improve the value of the mother and of the father to their family.

It has been thought that the child is born good and that all education should aim at preventing his straying from his first goodness. Jean-Jacques has explained to us in *Emile*—in the person of Emile—how he was born perfect, and how all the bad that was to be found in him was the work of men. But Jean-Jacques has merely described for us the state of soul and the inner experience of a pathological temperament, of a neuropath suffering from delusions of persecution, and his experience was but a caricature of that of humanity. The interior development of Jean-Jacques bears the marks of his profound lack of affective qualities, the absence of any gift for sympathy, and his conception of the child, born good but having become bad through the coldness of others, which is explained at length in the *Confessions*, (with more richness than in *Emile*), is the projection of his own frigidity into the soul of another. The thesis of the child which has been born good and has become less good owing to the action of society, is above all the illusion of strange and inhuman temperaments, of paranoiacs who have never been able to see the love by which they are surrounded; it is the illusion of those who are blind to affection, who are always passing by loving-kindness without being aware of it, and who while begging in the most puerile fashion for compassion, nevertheless commit acts of revolting selfishness. Jean-Jacques abandoned his own child.

He was however the man who raised the question of education, and it was he who showed that it is a superhuman work. All gentle and loving hearts have been touched by the account of such misfortunes, just as they are affected by the unconscious cruelties of mothers, as described to us by learned teachers. But if we would follow this to the end, we shall find that the whole matter can always be summed up in a few words: the injustice of adults and of men towards a child, and certain claims in favour of the child. There is a complete, pseudo-learned theory of teaching which would inform us that a child is altogether a different being from an adult, and that we only succeed in doing it harm. It is true that the wave of claims which has been made in favour of children has done much good, in the sense that their general conditions of life among adults has been improved. But there is no reason for believing that the good which has been done proves that there is an antagonism between children and grown-ups, that it proves the need for eliminating everything which might cause a shock to their egotistical little souls, the need to create a special children's world, different from that of the adults, and one from which the difficulties by which adults are assailed have been excluded. The Rousseau attitude, which has been cried up and developed under so many different forms, in which moreover one can find a number of excellent things, and which tends to represent real parents as possessed of powers over the child to which they have no right, as usurpers who should have a sort of shame on account of the conditions which nature imposes on them, and who are normally incapable of understanding their children, is inspired by a wrong attitude from the start. The childhood of the man who wrote *Emile* was not a normal childhood: this man had nothing in him which would ever make him loved, and his life displays for us the drama of those pitiful creatures whom everything wounds, who fail to recognise love because they do not know what loving means, who shut themselves up in a state of painful reaction, and who die as hypochondriacs, imagining themselves persecuted, fierce in their integrity but weak in will. In his book and in his writings we no doubt find the elements of the drama of every childhood, and though we are not familiar with the deformed vision of the world which Rousseau gives us, yet we hoist the experience of all children to the level of this morbid vision; we start believing that if all others do not write their memoirs in the style of Rousseau, it is because everyone has not the same sensibility or the same genius, even that all children suffer the harm which he suffered and which was his martyrdom, and have done so from all eternity. This is an error: only morbid temperaments, which are characterized by the intrusion of an unconscious and ungovernable egoism into their lives, take the same view of the world, and, apart from the question of literary and intellectual richness, they write just like him. The problem, as put by Rousseau, of one condemned, like all those diseased minds who resemble him, to remain alone and misunderstood in the very midst of friendship, is badly put.

The question of knowing whether a child is born good or bad is meaningless. It could have some meaning if a child was born self-sufficient, and could for instance be abandoned in a forest. But a child is born in such a state of weakness and dependence, a state which lasts for such a long time, that when for the first time it is able to make a decision of its own free will, the main lines of its personality have already been completed, for *the intervention of others has never ceased* to be intimately bound up with its development.

A child is born with a certain capacity for intellectual and emotional reactions; this capacity is characterized by a constitutional and evolutionary element at all stages of life, an element closely connected with the state of the body and the parental heritage. This capacity is however merely potential, for it is only able to react when in human surroundings, and the first reaction of a child bears at the same time the imprint of its own temperament and also of its surroundings. This should help us to understand how useless and foolish it is to imagine that we can calculate the amount of influence exercised by surroundings or direct it in its details; it proves that in the natural order no sensible technique can be worked out which is capable of replacing life itself. The fact is that when a child is born a being comes into the world to mix with other living beings. A child does not stop the life going on around it, indeed it cannot be stopped, for it has to live.

And precisely because life continues, because new-born children and infants are so susceptible to influence and so frail, is it necessary then to shield them from those displays of feeling which would seem to have no value, and to try and create artificially perfect surroundings around them, only taking into account the immediate needs of their childish personalities?

Viewed in the abstract, the discussion could be prolonged indefinitely, with excellent reasons to be advanced both for and against. I think, however, that there is no single reply to this question, and that we must set out to comply with what the facts teach us.

IV

The most striking thing, when we approach the question of how human beings are formed, is the irreplaceable rôle played by the normal family circle, the father and mother, the brothers and sisters. This does not appear directly, but we are able to show what the results are when it is absent.

Children who have been brought up by an aunt, by a grandmother or by their sisters (whether as orphans or because they belonged to a large family), or have spent their childhood in an orphanage, whether religious or secular, will bear the marks of their upbringing for the rest of their lives, apart from certain exceptional cases in which their adoptive parents have been able to rise above their elementary, spontaneous reactions.

To state the matter exactly, these children always lack the same thing. It can be summed up as follows: their feelings and affections are exclusively set on their rights and not on their duties. Such children seem to be strangely preoccupied with justice and as, owing to the lack from which they suffer, they look on every question of duty as involving an injustice, if the least moral conflict arises, they consider themselves injured and misunderstood and react accordingly. They tend to have a very perfect understanding of good and evil, which will be in proportion to the development of their intelligence, but this understanding is of a purely abstract kind; when it is a question of determining what is good and what is bad in regard to their conduct, then what is pleasant becomes the good, and what is unpleasant the bad. This tendency, which is to be found in every mind, in their case becomes so general that it completely deforms the sense of their moral reactions.

Their capacity for love is limited to being loved, and of being loved only in so far as this love does not deprive them of some other gratification. They themselves do not love, though they often are wheedlers. We may say that their capacity for loving is completely undeveloped and that their affective life has been unable to emerge from the stage of infantile egoism. This incapacity for love, and especially for generous love, extends to people, to animals and to things. It is characterized by their indifference to the suffering they cause to others (although in certain cases they can be sensitive to the sufferings which others cause to each other) and by indifference to the love which others may have for them; their lack of affection as regards everything which is not themselves, and themselves at that actual moment, leaves them indifferent as to the future; their reactions are always to the present, which makes them socially and professionally unstable.

Their moral incompleteness can turn them into thieves or the equivalent of thieves (parasites), and at the same time into those who are socially dissatisfied, that is to say reformers, whether great or small, whose claims are not those of unselfish generosity, but of those who wish to share in the results of other people's efforts; their social outlook is not that of those who share but of those who dispossess. This is indeed a good test for assessing the true value of all social reformers.

This picture is to be found again apart from all personal and hereditary failings. As a general rule it is not love which these human beings have lacked, though this may be the case; nor is it usually due to a lack of intelligence, of morality, or of devotion, or the product of artificial surroundings or caused by anything outside the family. And yet the fact remains and there is no escape from it. It is that, in normal family surroundings, there is something special, a collection of forces which, apart from all conscious attempts at teaching, play a part that is essentially formative and moral. If the quality of the human beings produced by the family is not necessarily always good, we can nevertheless state that the percentage of failings within is negligible when compared with the almost constant failures outside the family.

It is not therefore in mere submission to tradition and custom that we should consider the family as an indispensable element in social life, and in what we are considering here, education. It is a matter of simple submission to an undoubted fact of experience, which has been observed thousands and thousands of times: a normal, decent family provides the ideal and necessary surroundings for successful education.

V

On philosophical and above all on biological grounds this goes without saying. In every species of animal the young receive from their parents all the assistance necessary for their protection and upbringing. This is a true truism. And yet, when we state it, we do so in order to draw attention to a fundamental biological condition: even among animals the upbringing and, if you will, at the same time the education of the young is a labour of love. It will certainly be said that it is a blind and instinctive love, connected with some transient organic modification, but it is none the less true that it is love, and we know the pitiful sadness of birds whose young ones have been stolen, the tenderness of wild animals towards their young and their courage in defending and preserving them. This does not however appear to be a pure love, and it is enough to have observed the life of a nest of young birds, or of a litter of young cats, and the behaviour of their parents, to have felt that these birds and these cats would have been the better for being brought up differently; we shall have been tempted to teach these animals something about education, and have noticed that, in spite of the love which the parents undoubtedly show, yet they have preserved what we may call their defects and their insufficiency. We would not distribute the food as it is done by a swallow or a sparrow, which remain so insensible to the appeals of the little creature which we find so moving, and we would like to give a good scolding to the cat for her careless indifference in replying to her little ones. But, in spite of everything, as long as the upbringing lasts, the parents will not react to the allurements of the little ones as they would to any stimulus coming from other sources, and for a long time they show infinite tolerance, which becomes progressively less as the little ones grow up.

So much is this the case that we may say that parental love produces devotion to the little ones, a devotion to be found at no other period in the lives of animals and that this devotion co-exists with all the insufficiency of the affections (in comparison with ourselves) of the animals observed, and which has no effect on their behaviour outside the nest; finally this love suspends, in regard to their young, the aggressive and positively selfish reactions which the parents retain in reference to other things, and which they gradually recover towards their descendants as the latter grow up.

Now, these lines have not been written with a view to laying down a scarcely flattering parallel, but in order to stress the fact that biologically, among living beings whom we would look upon as prone to follow their organic urges blindly, the definitely parental period brings with it within the family group, *profound and unexpected modifications both in behaviour and character*, modifications without which nothing would be possible; that in consequence, in the order of creation, there are reasons for believing that the birth of a child is accompanied by certain interior phenomena in the parents, phenomena which are favourable to the development of the child, and are exclusively confined to the parents; that no place in the world, other than the family, is awaiting this child, and can give it what the family gives.

There is, furthermore, a definite question behind all this: how is it that a grandmother, who may seem to have more wisdom and experience than a mother, is not suited to bringing up a child?

Why, with all the resources of scientific education is no institution whatever, even where knowledge and devotion are not lacking, able to train a soul as it should be trained, whereas any simple woman who is endowed with average devotion, can, within the family circle, almost always succeed in this work? Why is it not desirable to see the family and the family education of children replaced by immense nurseries, and later by boarding-schools or scientific educational establishments, which would be expected to be more efficient than the father and mother?

One is at times tempted to think that the ideal of a large number of hygiene experts would be to confide all newly-born babies to some aseptic institution for as long as possible. There are such establishments connected with most maternity hospitals; the children are looked after in groups and it is said to work very well. But the children are not really weaned from their mothers, and this mechanisation of life lasts for a few weeks at the longest. There is a considerable difference between this rational and hygienic manner of looking after and protecting the children and a conception according to which, in order to free the mother, the children should be brought up like this all the time. There are already

B

nursery schools where mothers leave their children on the way to the factory, which is no doubt better than a complete separation. We are always shown fine establishments, airy and clean, and the collective mother is careful and attentive. But what of the rest? And who has the care of these little souls? And who will think, when they have grown up, that they could have become different from what they are? Who, however, will not agree that it is better, if the mother must go to work away from home, that she should confide her child to the nursery school or to the kindergarten, rather than to the caretaker, or to a neighbour, or even just leave it alone in the house. We here touch on the drama of existence. Have these children the right to a real mother, or not?

Is it necessary to have had a real mother and a real family?

If the hygiene expert is already tempted to suspect the mothers, the scientific pedagogue in his turn usually does not hesitate to say that the family is merely a centre of educational infection.

The matters for which these educational experts blame the family are not always fanciful. But in the same way that an intelligent mother of a family can learn in a few days elementary hygienic notions in regard to her children, and this happens often enough, so can the family circle make themselves acquainted with certain conceptions, they can learn them and bring them to perfection, and the small amount which the educationalists know of value can bear fruit perfectly in the midst of a normal family. Educational science is a far less effective science than is usually believed and its development is far from being satisfactory; it may, in certain cases, draw attention to some rude error, but at the present time it is not in a position to give exclusive directions, for it cannot claim that it has sufficient knowledge on the subject of the formation of personality. Educationalists must continue to study the facts, and for a long time, and should be very careful about intervening.

Hygiene and educational science are both indispensable, but they cannot be described as *raisons d'être* in themselves; they are means but not ends, and we must be careful to keep them in their right place. At the present time, in western countries, there is no genuine attempt to make them replace the family, but words are used all too often which would seem to say that the family is only there for the care of the children, as if everything had been done for a child once its hygiene was assured and it had been given its lessons. Now, necessary as these things may be, they are not the essential; the essential consists in that extraordinary combination of things which makes up a moral, affective and intellectual personality.

This personality is bound up with both the past and the future, and also with a definite conception of life; it has its place in a special spot in the world and in time, which is its centre of love, impregnated with the mystery of the family, through which it sees, understands, loves or hates; this is a definite spot which the "I" will continue to inhabit throughout its life, without knowing it, in which its consciousness will have its roots, and from which it will pass judgement though it be at the other end of the world . . . .

And since the family is quite lacking in educational science, and since it even obtains this result without knowing it and without noticing that it has been obtained, an extraordinary thing must have happened when the child was born; since such marvellous results are not obtained without their being a reason for them, there must then have been some unsuspected richness within the paternal home; since a work is completed in this home, which could not be carried out anywhere else in the world, there must have been some spell within it which accompanied the arrival of the child-king.

VI

At this point physiologists tell us that a mother's love is no more than a snare of the species, merely the product of adapted glandular function, furthermore that it can be produced experimentally in the laboratory, and that after all it is just an organic and instinctive expression, blind, in itself of no value, and of no importance. Physiologists say this quietly and with the somewhat artless irony of a chemist discussing the things of the spirit. But in their wake come the enemies of the family, of maternity and of family education. They take up the same arguments, use them to the full, endow them with considerations proper to a free-thinker, and present maternity, the maternal instinct and family education of children as expressions of a lower form of life, on a par with blind submission and the ways of animals. This facile banter is by no means confined to those who are in revolt against all moral organisation of the world, and there are many occasions when we have heard the maternal instinct laughed at, though certainly in a mild way, even by ecclesiastics, in proportion as what they are pleased to call this instinct is opposed to their ways of seeing things.

We must try and bring things into focus. When physiologists discover the necessary and sufficient conditions for the appearance of the maternal instinct, they have discovered a mechanism, but nothing more. It also confirms what has been established since the earliest days of humanity, that maternal love answers to something surpassing human personality, to some pre-established order from which the individual is physiologically unable to separate himself, and corresponds, according to the universal expression, to an instinct.

Let the physiologist continue his experiments in the knowledge that his discoveries confirm a belief, that they support age-old evidence, and strengthen the natural position of the family.

VII

The psychologists of our day make certain definite claims. A certain number of them, even among those teaching in the universities, do not yet know what human anguish is, and have never thought that it has a part to play. We shall perhaps do well not to waste our time on them; they have never really seen sick people, and speak of all these questions as if they were discussing philosophy; their being blind to all affective problems would not matter so much were it not that, as psychology is gaining ground socially, they are destined to have an unfortunate influence, treating children and mankind as casually as if they did not exist.

Others have come to know about anguish in the metaphysics of psychoanalysis. They talk a lot about it, and make it an essential matter, which indeed it is, but they see it as an undesirable factor in life and their aim, as indicated in the title of one of their books, is to create a type of man who will be without anguish. The first group do not take it into account, and the others wish to suppress it. It goes without saying that pathological anxiety reactions should be suppressed, but it is important that anguish and pathology should not be treated as synonymous. A certain propensity for anguish is the condition for all moral life; it is the factor which keeps the individual organically connected with reality, with life as it is lived. This propensity for anguish is the element by which the external world has the whip-hand of us, and to liberate anyone from all anguish, were such a thing possible, even for a psychoanalyst, would be to turn him into a being so enmacipated, so prone to live egocentrically, that he would become monstrous. Most psychoanalysts have allowed themselves to be psychoanalysed. They have thus acquired the technique and the "benefit" of the method, and the greater number of them have become unsociable and so aggressive that they constitute a real menace for those around them. All problems of behaviour, all conflicts which have to be resolved by an effort at adaptation and one of the will, are presented by them as anomalies, pathological tendencies, repressions and complexes. I would in general accuse the Freudian doctrine of never having regarded mankind except from the angle of absolutely egocentric behaviour.

In the same way the psychoanalysed subject may be blamed for having acquired a completely egotistical mentality, one that is at the same time rationalising and paranoiac, shall we say, and which could be described as having been castrated in its affective life. It is obvious that certain forms of psychoanalysis can help an individual to see clearly into himself and to discover some indefensible attitude beneath the appearances of strict or ultra-moral behaviour; but we may assume that the number of persons sufficiently gifted to undergo a purely psychoanalytical education without too much danger is very small. Such an education usually reinforces the aggressiveness of the subjects to an excessive extent, an aggressiveness which sometimes shows itself solely by a refusal to take into consideration the real personalities of other people. Psychoanalysis is a distinguishing feature in the education of young Americans and it would seem that, thanks to this release from all complexes, social relations are greatly simplified, and resemble the relations of robots. They are only easy if you ask for nothing and expect nothing.

VIII

When they read certain books on educational science, parents or educators take fright. It suddenly seems to them that their task as parents is superhuman, that it is not possible for them to carry it out without doing irreparable harm. We shall do well to keep a fundamental truth in our heads: the essential part of a personality is what it inherits. This shows itself in two principal ways, on the one hand, in the value presented at a given moment by each of the elements which we separate for the purpose of studying them, such as the general intellectual level and the factors on which this general intellectual level depends, among which are the emotional life and that of the affections, which provide the fundamental structure of man's relation with the outside world; on the other hand the succession and the regularity of the awakening of certain aspirations and interests, so that there may be an important hereditary failing in the premature awakening of some special form of sensitiveness or emotional reaction, or in the late appearance of certain functions of the affections. It is not merely a physiological question or one to do with the hormones, (the matter is well known in this domain), but something far more subtle which still remains secret. In brief, heredity reveals itself as much in the state as in the way in which the essential factors appear.

The absence of complete and stable family surroundings will invariably tell on the formation of the most gifted and best balanced child, and will reveal itself by disturbances in social stability and an incompletely developed moral sense. To speak the truth, the absence of family surroundings constitutes so serious a disturbance that the formation of the profoundest structures is bound to be affected by it. But in well adjusted family surroundings, in which a tolerably good atmosphere reigns, it is not easy to produce really serious disturbances. We may also think that during the course of education all the essential faults have been committed, which are likely to lead to aberrations. Now, the contrary is the case; the normal child will put up a resistance to many troubles before it will begin to react with neurotic aberrations, and we may regard it as a rule that only the child which already has some defect will react with such deviations. The latter will choose from among the mistakes made during his education those which strengthen its latent dispositions or correspond to its weaknesses. A normal child, on the contrary, will be balancing one thing against another, straightening things out and adjusting them, day by day. It, no doubt, also bears the marks of that education but it bears these marks in a way which characterize it without ruining it. On the other hand, in the case of a child with biological defects, the most perfect education will have unfortunate results, since it is impossible to provide such a child with the elements corresponding to its morbid requirements.

We quite often hear psychologists or educationalists explaining the hatred felt by a child for its parents or for one of them as due to some fault on the part of the latter, to clumsiness or lack of understanding, to injustice or even to ill-treatment. Such ideas have no connection with reality. A normal child will always be attached to its mother, even if she is unworthy of its affection. If it hates her, then it is because it has biological defects. In this matter psychoanalysts seem to me to have missed the point. This does not mean that there are no complexes or conflicts, or that it is not necessary to do everything possible to minimise them. Serious family hatreds are only to be found in neuropathic types, and such hatreds would exist even if the father and mother were perfect. When hatred or resentment reach a point where it appears necessary to call in a doctor or psychologist, then there is clearly a lack of balance and a neuropathic condition.

CHAPTER TWO

The Child and its Environment

I

For many people the question of environment is no more than one of distinguishing those environments which are good from those which are bad, these being estimated according to certain social standards. Such a conception is by no means worthless and it has already been of considerable service.

We should however be mistaken in trying to simplify things as much as this. While we must not underestimate the importance of an environment, nevertheless we should not lose sight of the influence exercised by other factors, when studying the formation of a personality. Now, these other factors can easily become confused with the environment itself. Suppose that a child is brought up in a slum, amid poverty, destitution, promiscuity, blows, and the most wretched sort of examples; in such a case we may certainly speak of an unsatisfactory environment. But people are all too often unaware that there are many people living in slums who do not wish to leave them, or would immediately turn some attractive home which was offered them into a slum. For such parents, their life in a slum is a form of social expression, the way in which they come to maturity, the mark of an inferior mentality. If this inferior mentality can sometimes be explained by a period of poverty or by certain individual difficulties, it is far more often the result of an intellectual and moral inferiority, which is transmitted from father to son like the shape of the forehead, the colour of the eyes and the organic characteristics.

In consequence, if a child is born into such an inferior environment, not only is it born into very unfavourable conditions for its education, but it will probably be born endowed with a moral and mental outlook of such a kind, that when it grows up this environment will seem to be the most suitable.

Our study of environment must thus never be limited to a superficial examination, but must be complete, taking into account the mental quality of the parents, how far their personalities correspond with their environment, also taking into account the qualities they possess because they are human, and how far these are likely to have been transmitted to their children.

To make this study of the environment complete, we must not merely be as exact as possible in first-hand investigations, but must also take into account the general significance of the environment.

We shall then be able to distinguish the different aspects, or at least three ways of looking at them.

II

We meet first of all with an environment that is *imposed*, and cannot be avoided, one that is normally bound up with the family; such an environment acts as a rule on a child before its moral consciousness has been formed, and it is unconscious of what is taking place; this state lasts from birth till the time comes to go to school. It has an all-powerful effect and leaves its mark on all later development.

Whether or no this environment has a great human value, a child must undergo its influence and will conform to it. We must here understand the word conform as meaning acceptance on general lines, and in no sense meaning that there will never be any conflict between a child and those around it. It is, really, quite normal that there should be a state of conflict between a being and its environment.

This family environment in no sense ceases to exert its influence when a child goes to school, indeed this influence continues indefinitely, but the child's outlook is broadened and new and very important elements are introduced; from then onwards the environment is one of the family combined with school. This new combination is by no means a mere placing two atmospheres side by side, but is itself one complete whole in which the fusion is brought about by the personality of the child.

We can speak then of an environment which is *discovered*, one which stretches from the age of going to school to that of puberty at least, which acts no doubt through unconscious influences, but which the whole time elicits conscious efforts at adaptation, efforts which become more and more numerous as the child grows up. Family and school each provide an environment, but they are environments with different systems, which require adaptations, and set the affections in motion. The family environment has in a sense been decreed by fate, but the school has already become a recurrent element. It will be no doubt chosen by the parents, but even then it will be something quite different from their ideas and their way of life; in certain circumstances it may even happen that the mental outlook of the school may be quite different from that of the parents, or even opposed to it. Schooling is something which takes place outside the family, and it will allow a child either to develop within the moral framework which is already there, or else to free itself from this, if the teaching of the school finds aptitudes or dispositions in its mind which in the family circle were in an undeveloped stage or maybe were definitely opposed; or else a child may dig itself into the family way of life, denying itself all development, because its school imagines that it lacks certain dispositions or that these are only indifferently and insufficiently developed.

Under the influence of the school a child will thus be able partially to escape from its family environment, as long as it has enough constitutional mental resources. If this environment is of inferior quality, and if the child is constitutionally also of inferior quality, the act of digging itself into the environment provides it with a sheet-anchor and will seem to be a form of order; it will develop within these narrow limits in harmony with the poor quality of its surroundings. When we have studied this case and the environment in which the child in its turn will have formed around it, it will be very important to know if it had the chance of escaping from its relations, if it went to school with anyway a minimum of opportunity; if that is the case, the fact of having returned to its point of departure will reveal its fundamental incapacity. But if it has not had the chance to get away, the fact that it has remained in a lower grade will prove nothing, anyway from the *a priori* standpoint.

It can finally happen that, though born in normal family surroundings, a child may be insufficiently gifted to develop normally; this may be due to passing organic difficulties, or it may be the mark of some permanent deficiency. In that case the school becomes a form of life from which it must escape at any cost, and as long as it lives in an environment of poor quality, this return to the family will take place without attracting attention; in normal circumstances, however, this exclusive turning back to the family circle, that is to say a turning back to a life of ease not without a certain laziness, is bound to cause a certain conflict; when a child refuses to adapt itself to a school, it is usually no more than the social aspect of a certain inadequacy, but it is expressed in the form of a real unsociability.

It goes without saying that blemishes in the character, the affections and the emotions play here as important a rôle as do simple intellectual deficiencies, and one can well understand how from this time onwards any lack of balance will be noticeable. The more normal the family, so much the more noticeable will this lack of balance be, and the family will be the more likely to be disturbed by certain manifestations or any unusual requirements; in a family with blemishes, however, this lack of balance will be far less noticeable, being no more than a form of activity well known in the family atmosphere.

We are thus led to understand that environment does not mean merely the place inhabited, a way of life or external social customs, but that it also includes the intrinsic qualities of parents and their offspring. We shall also grasp how closely the problem of environment overlaps those of heredity and natural constitution.

This leads us on from an environment which is imposed and inevitable to one which is discovered, and then on to one *which is sought for and chosen*. In the case of an adult this may mean an environment in which he resigns himself to live, or one which has been chosen deliberately, but however this may be we are concerned with a way of life which is the self-expression of the individual.

This resignation to living in a certain environment, or the choice of one, is in the first place a result, a result revealing the formation which has been received; the latter will have been produced by the imposed environment, then by that which was found and by the reactions of the personality. The environment in which an adult lives will thus produce a state of stagnation (whatever may be the actual value of the environment itself) of regression, of advance or of renunciation. It must always be appraised as the environment from which the individual has emerged. From the educative point of view, an environment which may seem to be inferior, but which may indeed vary from a wretched slum to one of considerable comfort, is far more interesting than easy surroundings in which there is eventual deterioration owing to some inner lack.

When we speak of a family as worthy to receive and educate children, we are thinking of one of moderate means, which may perhaps rise a little in the social scale. If we study such a family we shall come to understand what happens in stagnant or retrogressive families. As has been pointed out, children, from the time when they reach the school age, have the chance of separating themselves to a certain extent from their environment, till they end up as adults able to make their own choice or else to resign themselves to their circumstances; in consequence, the fact that a child is born in certain surroundings or in a certain place in the world, in such a street or such a village, is not a mere matter of chance, but a form of expression of the family stock from which it is sprung and which it will tend to resemble, without however being all the time the slave of its origin.

Environment is not something absolute, it is the result of a combination of causes, a state of equilibrium which arises at a particular moment of time between society and one of its cells; I am almost tempted to say that at one particular moment it is a social attitude. Now, this "attitude," which expresses itself in one way from the social point of view, expresses itself in another way from the intra-family point of view, but qualitatively these are the same. From this comes the importance and the complexity of the notion of the family circle and its surroundings.

A child is born, then, into a family which behaves towards society in a certain way, which thus constitutes a circle and its surroundings, because it has certain ways of looking at life and things, and a certain way of reacting to them. In the normal order of things a child is bound to submit, during the richest period of its life, to these surroundings which are imposed on it, and it is to our interest to see what happens during these first five years of its life.

III

Some of our observations may seem to be out of contact with all reality. When they read what we have to say, many parents will imagine that we are not describing the life of all children and certainly not the life of their own. They forget that they very soon see in their children only an assortment of external qualities and that certain thoughts and certain reactions which are obstinately shielded from their eyes nevertheless have a directing influence in their children's lives. They forget that what they know of their children is but a very small part of the reality, and often enough only corresponds very slightly with their real personalities. They remain unaware that what they do not know about their children is in fact their most important part, that which separates them from them, and cannot be communicated to them. Some parents are even convinced that their children hold no secrets from them, and make no small efforts to preserve this illusion. They only succeed in causing their children to wear a mask which is all the more impenetrable because they insist on believing it is the real truth. Our aim here is to try and show exactly what the parents fail to see, which is nevertheless at the base of every personality.

IV

A child will be born. Since it gave the first suspicion of life, it has either been blessed or cursed. The whole of its life will be marked by its father's first reflexions on hearing the news, by the start of anguish or joy on the part of the mother. And, with their cold severity, statistics inform us that during the first years of their existence two illegitimate children die for every one that dies brought up in a family. But between these two extremes there are many legitimate children who experience the distress and abandonment of their less fortunate brothers and sisters.

This child which is about to come to birth may be the eldest, the second, the third or the last of some household; it will have been preceded or will be followed by some girl or boy, and the place which it will occupy either after or before a sister or a brother will influence it profoundly. Nobody will be able to change this. It may be born in a sunny house or a dark corner: its first glance may follow the marvellous mobility of leaves and branches, the harmony of living and supple flowers, or it may be fixed on the sleepy deadness of roofs . . . its parents will not often have been able to choose. But there is one thing which can be avoided with a newborn child: the misfortune of not being the boy or the girl which was expected. I am fully aware that, in numerous cases, a disappointment of this sort does not diminish the love with which the child is received. This is especially so in the case of a first child. But when a number of children have already been born, and for some obscure reasons it has been decided that a son or a daughter is wanted, it becomes more difficult to accept the fact with resignation, if these hopes are disappointed. It can happen for a mother or a father to take a dislike to such a child, or in better cases their instinctive movement of love is hindered or simply inhibited. It can also happen that one of the parents whom fortune has satisfied at the expense of the hopes of the other, secretly makes this a personal affair, sincerely imagining that this child will never be loved like the others, which will lead eventually to one of them protecting the child, spoiling it and drawing it away from the authority of the other partner, who is felt to be lacking in fondness: this can cause the moral ruin of the child.

Doctors can all too often become quite innocently accomplices in this attitude if they attempt to predict, more or less scientifically, what the sex of the child will be. They are frequently in error, and their authority as doctors will only have made a disappointment harder to bear. We cannot too strongly recommend parents and doctors not to think they know better than the laws of biology: on an average 106 boys are born for every 100 girls.

If the Christian names are decided on beforehand they should be *of both sexes* and if, in spite of everything, the parents have each to resign themselves to stating their desire clearly, then the father should have the generosity to agree with the wishes of the mother. The latter will forget far more quickly, and once the disappointment has taken place her one concern will often be that everything has worked out for the best. But the best thing is to avoid any form of calculation as there will then be no chance that the child, having learnt a few years later of the hopes which birth failed to fulfil, will end by saying, in the course of some educational disagreement: "They have never really loved me, I have never been forgiven for not being a girl!" This phrase may seem to be of little importance, but the state of mind which it expresses can develop under a wide variety of forms in numbers of children, and is quite capable of warping the whole of their lives.

There are also all too many cases where a child is loved exaggeratedly, and at the expense of the others, because it happened to be a boy or a girl just at the time when its parents were hoping for one. What are we to think of those who go on pilgrimages and make novenas, and in general behave in a puerile fashion, asking God to change the laws of nature, because they already have two boys, or because they would have difficulty in providing dowries for three daughters? In this matter we must trust to the ways of life, and such preliminary calculations are, unfortunately, in most cases dictated by selfish rather than generous motives.

It is strange that for so many parents the question of the sex of the child they are awaiting should alone seem of importance. There is a far more serious question and a much more legitimate concern, which can at times arouse no small anxiety: will the child be a healthy one? It has been said that there is no couple sufficiently healthy for there to be any certainty that their offspring will be satisfactory in every respect. Apart from their normal concern with the coming event, the one useful thing that parents can do before the birth of a child is to do all they can with a view to its health. We know how in France there are what are known as Sunday children (*enfants du dimanche*) which have been conceived when the father was under the influence of drink. A father should never have to ask himself, when faced with some irregularity in the child which he has called into the world, whether some adventure or some over-convivial evening, which he now calls to mind, may not have contributed to this. The same may be true of maternal excesses: with most mothers alcoholic excesses are unusual, it is in most cases one of overwork, of extreme fatigue, even of exhaustion, and of the pregnancies coming too close together.

If the child is not normally constituted, if the fundamental cells have been impeded in their formation, every attempt at education will be in vain, every hope will be disappointed, all sacrifices will be of no avail.

V

A long time before the birth is due parents turn their thoughts to the question of names.

Names are one of those fundamental elements which leave their mark on the destiny of human beings. There must be nothing in these names which gives any idea of backwardness or inferiority, such as would produce in the personality of its bearer some needless complex. For the same reason, but as it were in the opposite sense, no extraordinary or pretentious name must be chosen. Just as a child should not have, on account of its name, any humiliating or depressing thoughts, at the same time there should be nothing in its name to give it a quite uncalled-for sense of superiority. The custom of choosing a name from among the saints of the calendar is very wise, and when, in order to distinguish their children from the common run of mortal men, parents turn to foreign names—some of the Slav and Nordic ones are very poetic— thus giving to a child a name which is very beautiful, but which, not being in use amongst us, tends to isolate its bearer in a slightly disdainful originality, they encourage the all too prevalent tendency amongst us to imagine we are different from other people.

In fact, when unsuitable names are given to children, it is often in order to please the godparents. In certain cases the choice of godparents can be very important, often more important than the choice of a Christian name, and it has been said that some children are more like their godparents than their real parents.

This way of seeing things, which is widespread in the notions of popular wisdom, is no doubt somewhat exaggerated; but nevertheless it is in accordance with a very precise idea, that of the rôle which god- parents should play in children's lives, as models who should be imitated. In the country especially, godparents enjoy certain prerogatives in regard to their godchildren, and children find in them certain types of people who are prepared to spoil them a little, and sometimes to defend them, while on their side the parents are often all too apt to flatter the godparents from ulterior motives. Children are by nature imitative, and will naturally be more inclined to imitate their godparents than anybody else, if the latter enjoy a special prestige in their eyes.

The choice of godparents is made according to certain family customs which have to be observed; but, apart from that it can happen, especially in large families, that a godparent has to be found. People are only too ready to choose someone who is interesting, or well off, from whom material support may be expected or anyway a favourable mention in the will. This interesting godparent may often be an unusual person, who perhaps has not married and has lived avariciously, or on the other hand with luxury and ostentation. The parents will admit with a certain definiteness, and more or less consciously, that they must be on good terms with these godparents, and will encourage the children to flatter them. They will start by giving the godparent's name to the newlyborn child, and thus Christian parents introduce into the life of their child, before it is capable of the smallest thought, a complete programme of servility, even of deceit, which may undermine the foundations of the good advice and even the good example which they should be able to give.

CHAPTER THREE

The First Fixations

I

The child is thus, even before its birth, absorbed by the family atmosphere, and its life is set in a certain direction. It already bears, from that time onwards, a very noticeable social and moral impress. This impress is the expression of certain tendencies which are deeply ingrained in its parents.

It is all too often imagined that a child passively receives the form which it is desired it should have as if it was but wax. This is only very partially true. A child is first of all a complex product of heredity; from this it receives the shape of its body, its physical appearance, its organic qualities or defects, and at the same time certain general mental tendencies. Among these mental tendencies we find in the first place a certain degree of intelligence.

This latter will enrich the mind which will accumulate, according to the degree of instruction received, a greater or lesser number of ideas. But however considerable may be the knowledge which any individual mind can acquire, the understanding of things which its owner can achieve will only reach a certain degree of perfection, in proportion to the quality of its intelligence. If there is no limit to the number of things which can be learnt, nevertheless there is a definite limit to the extent to which they can be understood, a qualitative limit which no amount of education can overcome. No matter what is done, a mediocre intelligence will only understand things in a mediocre way. To achieve an independent moral life requires a minimum of intelligence for which no amount of education is a substitute.

That which holds true of intelligence also holds true of the emotions and the passions. In this matter education has a very large rôle to play, in that it is able to modify the social and moral forms which are taken by these emotions and these passions, but it will remain without influence on the organism of which these are the expression. For example, the intensity and the lasting quality of the emotions is in a certain sense an organic phenomenon; the same is true of the fundamental passions and of the natural capacity of the individual for taking part, both in pain and in sorrow, in its environment and with the other people around.

This makes up a complete whole, which reveals itself as the new human being develops, but which exists prior to all education; its flowering will however take place in close connection with this education. That which conforms with the general tendencies of this new man will come to be fairly easily accepted, while that which is opposed to these tendencies will end in a compromise. The intelligence will greatly help towards achieving this compromise. Furthermore, the child will be more or less subject to the influence of the family in so far as its emotional life needs to be surrounded with sympathy in order to live or is indifferent to that sympathy, a fact which is essentially the result of heredity and on which education has very little effect. Now, there exists a wide range of degrees between the optimum and the minimum, and were there only the factor of variable sympathy between the members of a family, how different they would all be, even though they would have all evolved in the same atmosphere, and been reared by the same parents.

In reality, the family, from the time of the first manifestation of life, tends to take possession of the new arrival, and the latter is endowed with a personality of its own. What it will become later on will be the product of its constitutional personality and of its education, a mixture of compromise, of conformity, of reactions, of occasional lack of understanding. The ideal which the educators have in view will be further frustrated if the stock from which the child is sprung has in it a morbid streak, constantly producing unexpected reactions, and in the end sometimes making all efforts at education vain, impossible and even tragic.

When all is said, it would be a mistake to suppose that apart from the general tendency to monopolize, which at times may be shown in rather rough fashion, that nothing else takes place between the parents and the child.

II

That movement of pure love which the parental instinct brings about in the father and the mother when they first see the child can, unless they take care, become vitiated immediately; it can speedily become a form of self-satisfaction, and this also explains why parental love is apt to evolve in such strange ways.

There is in the first place one constant fact, and that is the physical likeness of the child to one or both of its parents. The parent which the child resembles most will probably have a particular sense of attachment to it, which is easily understood; this can strengthen parental love, but it may at the same time corrupt it, for it is caused by a form of self-satisfaction which may be definitely injurious. If one of the parents should indulge in self-love through the medium of the child, then how can he or she prevent themselves (though perhaps not altogether aware this is happening) from protecting the child from education itself, from those little punishments which are a minor tragedy in the life of children. If they give themselves up to this, they will soon end by loving nothing except their own reflection in the life of the child, and if, as often happens, the resemblances become modified with the course of years, if the features, the hair and the eyes become changed, if as they evolve they become like those of the other partner or become just a mixed type, then it is as if the child had disappeared and often enough this exaggerated love collapses with these organic changes, and even transforms itself into resentment. It can also happen, though this is a rarer case, that one of the parents, recognizing the others in the child, may in a sense try to translate conjugal love into the realm of paternal love, certainly a fairly rare event, but one which tends to be quite frequent in cases of widowhood, and which, we must stress, can be of no small danger.

It can also happen among parents that, in spite of an outer appearance of goodwill, there is a deep antagonism, perhaps never expressed, but existing in the form of a hidden conflict. Under such conditions, the fact of discovering in the child some trait which has a bearing on this conflict, will be quite enough to produce in one of the parents a kind of inner resistance, one which is obscure and stubborn and quite capable of preventing the parental instinct and love from revealing itself completely.

III

What has just been said of physical is even more true of moral characteristics. We should remember that parents do not know each other as they see themselves in their inner knowledge of themselves, and that though they may have been united by intimate affinities, yet it is above all by differences in the expression of their lives that they come to know each other, differences which can cause them a considerable amount of suffering. Now, we often consider as faults in another person what are really his reactions to his own personal faults of which we know nothing, and it is very easy for partners in marriage to have quite a false idea of each other, from which they are unable to escape, and which is really only the reflection of their relations with each other. Parents are inclined to transfer this incomplete knowledge of each other to their children: they will recognise qualities in them which they have failed to understand (that is to say, their own qualities which they have failed to understand) or, on the other hand, certain faults, which are to a large extent imaginary. They thus build up for themselves an untrue picture of the child, and will be all too inclined to behave in accordance with it. It is obvious that these essentially selfish preoccupations will have an adverse effect on the child's upbringing, if the parents are not sufficiently aware of them to repress them. The more parents differ from the normal type—whether owing to a genuine superiority, or, as is more often the case, owing to neuropathic tendencies—so much the more are these failures to understand likely to be both frequent and serious, and they will have their effect both on their love for and the education of the children.

In a general way it goes without saying that the less the moral formation of the parents has been developed, so much the more are such capricious tendencies likely to replace the true end of education. Finally, the family standard in a number of cases is of such a kind that no real attention is paid to the children, so that the latter develop in reaction against a collection of parental reflexes, of a thoroughly valueless type, and thus develop in a way by which they are most exposed to the effects of moral defects.

Parents must therefore take special care to preserve the purity of their love for their children, to keep it well apart from their cares and their personal complexes, not to make use of them in order to gain points, to justify themselves or even just to prove the faults of others. This would seem to require that the parents should have undergone a certain formation, that they should have a definite moral attitude; paternal love of this kind would be unlikely to produce anything of value, and could easily be used merely in the service of the parents themselves, with the child being used as no more than a means. On the other hand, in cases where the parents have been able to rise above themselves, they will be compelled to improve, to judge with greater tolerance and understanding, and through their mutual share in the upbringing of their children, they will come to know each other better and to have a higher appreciation of each other.

In short, there should be no idea of forming the child according to the difficulties experienced by the parents at the time, trying to make it resemble heaven knows what opportunist and probably contradictory ideal, with the mother pursuing one end and the father another, while they each imagine they are pursuing the ideal; both parents should be in agreement over some rule of life which will transcend them both, which will transcend all that is perfect in them, and will be out of reach of the blows which their failings will possibly, if not probably, aim at it. Both parents must be subject to a moral code, to the same moral and human ideals, they must pursue this consciously, without delaying too long where the road is rough. Besides, as we shall see a little later on, the child has the right not to be reproached for acting like its father or mother, and it also has the right that its parents should not impress on it certain ways of behaviour which are likely to give it the impression that it is predestined to behave in that way, by this very fact leading it to abandon the struggle against itself.

IV

Before we give the child up to love, may we be allowed to make one other suggestion. The parents have their interior life. They congratulate themselves on certain results which they have obtained in the course of their lives, while at the same time there have been reverses which they regret. This is bound to make them set a value on a special state of soul, while there will be certain habits which they will despise. Parents tend to have memories of inferior qualities in themselves to which they attribute the reverses which have taken place in their lives, and with these in mind they wish to train their children so as to arm them for the struggles of life. There are some qualities which they would wish to develop, and they would sometimes even seek to develop certain defects. Parents would do well to leave such ideas well alone. In most cases they are unaware of what really caused them to fail, and their weaknesses are frequently quite different from what they imagine. The idea of fulfilling themselves in their children will usually only lead to exaggerations and to errors.

In spite of everything, the family spirit will act in a very special way on the child, for the parents cannot be expected to become nameless and characterless teachers.

They will not be able to prevent their emotional life from seeping into their love, weaving a thousand strange links between the child and themselves, and thus producing a thousand different visions; it is precisely this which gives their love such unsurpassable richness. They will be able to prevent themselves from having a conscious desire to act or to love in a special way; they will not, however, be able to escape from those subconscious reasons which direct and organise the love of every human being within the limits of its moral code. The father will not love his son in the same way that he loves his daughter, and the same is true of the mother. Both parents, without being aware of the fact, will have a slightly different way of treating each child, and this from the earliest days. The voice, the colour of the eyes and the hair, the figure, the facial expression and the gestures, the whole pantomime of the emotions, these will all awaken special echoes in each parent, and will arouse suitable manifestations of love. The personality of a child begins by living in the looks of those who love it, or, to be more exact, begins by existing in what it can understand of the looks which follow it around. The looks given by its father and mother, and the various expressions accompanying them, play a very important part in the formation of an infant. Before it can work out anything analytically, roughly after it is past the age of one year, it has quite a different way of responding to paternal or maternal looks; at that time a child lives already under two forms, and is already known under two different aspects. A young child cannot live and develop normally without the communion of love of those faces and intimate glances, and because it needs those glances, which it ends by knowing very well, (when it is a few months old a child reacts to the most delicate distinctions in these glances, and indeed to any glance at all), it behaves well in consequence. In a normal family the continuity of these glances, of this spiritual communion, is assured, and it is from this that the kernel of the personality is formed.

Only the family can assure the permanence and the steadfastness of those intimate beings by which a child lives. Only the family can obtain for it, in a continuous and progressive manner, that complex of living affinities which its mother and father make up, a complex in which the child finds expression and feels that it finds expression, and of which its own personality will at a given moment become an expression. Neither the professional smile of a nurse, kind though this may be, though it is too often lacking in depth and in life, nor the continual changing of faces, can be compared with this intimate relationship of the life of the soul, always identical yet always evolving, which takes place in the family.

V

The affective formation, that is to day the organization of the life of the emotions, in a framework which will last, takes place in the early years.

In an artificial environment children become accustomed too rapidly to constant changes in their immediate surroundings, in the faces of their friends and in their amusements. As they never have time to become attached to anything, so do they cease to have any real regrets; they do not get into the way of loving anything, with the fear that they may lose this. Their emotional life does not become accustomed to anything definite, for everything around them is changing the whole time. They lack that long contact with things from which the true idea of time is able to emerge slowly.

This idea of time, which is so slow in forming and which is independent of the theoretical understanding of duration, has a rich moral content. It clearly does not exist by itself or for itself, but is in a sense a resultant, for it is already a product of the experience of life.

It is produced by the periodical return of certain quite important events, such as being taken into somebody's arms, of seeing a special face bending over with a special kind of glance, of knowing the pleasure of eating, of being held in a certain way; a child grows accustomed to being taken into the arms of a certain person, for, once the adaptation has been made, it will weep if anyone else lifts it up, solely because the impression received is not the same . . . It does not weep because anything disagreeable happens, but it has a disagreeable feeling, as the impression which it had grown to enjoy is replaced by another impression. It is clear that this does not take place consciously, but that is how the sense of regret first sets in. Tears will also teach it that they can constitute a language. Having first wept by reflex action, it will finish by weeping in order to recover a certain pleasure, or to obtain and to keep some object, or to attract the attention and the goodwill of the outer world.

However, mothers have not always time to spare and children have to learn to wait or else to ask in vain.

This is where grandmothers can do no small harm; they have often developed a rather childish affection for the little ones and lack the courage to let them cry. They can thus prevent their grandchildren from learning that their desires will not always be met in the same way, but instead they encourage them to live entirely in the present.

In the same way they form in them the habit of expecting the elements to obey them (those which concern the children are naturally the only reality for them) and prevent them from grasping how great is the power of external realities, or how these move and act quite independently of their desires and in spite of their tears or their rages.

In short, at the same time as a vague consciousness of duration comes into being, there is also consciousness that there is a certain succession and a certain order.

VI

This vague consciousness that there is a certain order is only possible where a child always lives in the same environment, among the same faces, keeping the same daily timetable, within the same framework. Otherwise, out of the jumble of external forces which interfere with its desires and its tendencies, nothing will emerge except a series of things disagreeable or pleasant, but which seem to lack any organization relating them together.

The child before long has a real life in relation with those things by which it is surrounded, and which it finds it can alter by means of its language, its tears, its cries, its smile. An infant ends by discovering a language of its own and also that there is a certain goodwill which some of its acts evoke while others fail to do so. The faces and eyes of its father and mother, their words and their caresses end by becoming expressions of that external reality, and their goodwill can only be obtained by acting in a certain way. Whereas the consciousness of the child is still only a vague possibility and no more than a hope, all this external organization of faces, caresses, of smiles and of food, informs it whether it is in friendly relations with these things or not, and requires from it a certain standard of behaviour. The moral sense is still far away; some years will have to pass by before it appears in the soul of this creature groping its way towards a clear consciousness of reality, but the deeper are its roots in the first glimpses of life, so much the better will it respond to the whole make-up of man; so much depends on how far the life of the first months and the first years has been submitted to the family order, to kindness and to love. This first, ordered picture of the world, this woof or canvas into which the future will wend its way, can only be obtained if the child has known the same people and things for some time, and has been sufficiently loved by them. The smile and goodwill of those around it which the child needs, and which it soon tries to win, will, if it succeeds in learning how to do so, only be able to lead it on to regular behaviour if it is itself ordered and regular.

After a year of life, a child has already been moulded by the regularity or the disorder of its hours of feeding and rest, by winning smiles or severe faces, according to the way in which it behaves. No moral sense can be formed amid disorder, dirt, instability, brutal actions and yells;

or simply amid indifference. Nor can it be formed amid a succession of smiles which are ever new and have no connection with its own world, amid things which do not correspond with its actions; this is what happens in families in which, on the pretext that the child is so young, it is con-considered that no discipline is needed.

The formation of a moral sense in children is inconceivable if they are brought up in unstable surroundings, in which there is no true love, or in a family in which the mother is so submerged by her children and her work that she has no time to smile at them, or in which the father pays no attention to them.

By the time that it is a year old a child is either accustomed to living in a state of dirt or else it cannot bear to be left dirty. It does not as yet know the difference between good and evil, but it is already able to howl so that its mouth and hands may be wiped, or that it may not be left to crawl about with a dirty napkin. The moral sense is still absent, but it will be difficult to produce it if a child has been left in a state of neglect during its early years. A child, when a year old, having grown accustomed to looking at a face and knowing its smiles, reacts profoundly to certain expressions, though these may be scarcely noticeable (I am not referring to coarse and rough expressions, for every child reacts against these at a much earlier date) and the possible delicacy of its conscience is already finding expression in this reaction.

Before it is two years old a child will have become extremely sensitive to disorder, if it has been brought up in tidy surroundings. It will cry, if the objects round it are out of place, if its bed is crossways, if things are lying about all round it, and this awareness of what is irregular, to which it gives definite expression, is the first expression of its interior order, of that which up to then has held for it the place of the moral law.

When a child cries so that the established order may be preserved around it, it cries because it needs that order, because its mental organization has reached the point that its emotional welfare requires that things should be arranged in a certain way in regard to itself.

Now, this need is a complex one, it has only come into being through an indefinite repetition of the same situations. And then, the physical order is in reality only one aspect of things, for there is the order of living beings which is far more important. By the time a child is two years old, the attitude of the living beings around it has become both fixed and known. There are its parents, its brothers and sisters, its family. There is the cat, the dog and its dolls. A child will love these beings and they have their own ways of behaving towards it, by which it learns that love is continuous and that it expresses itself. Just as it needs the physical order, so does it need this continuity of affection. All these beings which evolve around it and take an interest in it have their own special attitudes, and a child gradually develops a special way of behaving towards each one of them. It tries to use this behaviour as a means of attracting more attention, and thus language and mimicry and the language of acts are developed.

Parents will only need to take account of the language of acts. They should distrust all mimicry (looks, wheedling, mannerisms, flattery and crying) by which a child tries to escape from the obligation of imposing a real sacrifice on itself, if it would maintain or increase that affection of which from now on it stands in need.

And in proportion as they succeed in making the language of acts have the leading place in the development of the child, between the ages of eighteen months and four or five years, they will have laid the first foundations of decent behaviour. In proportion as they allow themselves to be taken in by pure mimicry, they will injure the development of its future moral character, indeed they may injure it for good and all. This is where certain unconfessed weaknesses may play a part, and where the moral sense of the parents and the level of their intelligence will permanently impress their action on the soul of the child.

A kind of instinct of rivalry between a child and its surroundings soon enters into all this and its upbringing, when seen from a certain angle, will appear as a succession of ceaseless efforts on its part to compel the services of those around it. These efforts will first be applied to animals, then to its brothers and sisters whose various personalities, as they quite naturally escape from these efforts, play as important a part in its formation as the parents.

VII

Superficial observers are apt to accept literally the conventional picture of the unmixed happiness of parents when confronted with their child. Nevertheless we should not forget that far more often than is usually believed and far more often than those concerned are prepared to admit, fathers have to make a real effort to accustom themselves to the presence of their child, indeed to the sovereignty of their child. In certain cases, when the father is not very intelligent and is perhaps neuropathic, he finds great difficulty in adapting himself and may display real jealousy, if not animosity, towards the newborn child; in other cases, while not owning it to himself, a father has to face genuine suffering, which only the most careful attention will reveal to him. When married love is not equally shared and the husband does not feel that he is accepted unconditionally, while he is himself very much in love with his wife, the affection shown by a mother for her baby, which, being partly compensatory, has about it a slight tone of exaggeration, can be bitterly resented by the father who feels that he is forsaken or set aside. Things no doubt seldom reach the point of definite explanations, because in most cases the wife becomes aware of what is happening before it is too late, and becomes better balanced. The little conflict thus set up can delay the full flowering of paternal love, or it may perhaps only arise because this same paternal love has been slow in forming. It is in any case a state of mind of no small subtlety, and can lead to plenty of difficulties. It can also happen, though more rarely, that the mother feels she has been dispossessed; this is almost always when she is lacking in maternal sense, in which case we are dealing with a thoroughly morbid case. We have only to allude to such things to take into account that the birth of the child in a clinic does not make them any easier.

VIII

To wind up this account, which is indeed poor enough when compared with the full richness of life, we can understand that it is of the first importance for the family circle to be stable and complete. In the light of these few ideas we can see how dangerous it is for births to come too close together, making it practically impossible for a mother to live among her own children and perhaps making the family atmosphere disagreeable and unhappy. This cannot be proved mathematically, and only a rough estimate can be given, but one might conclude that an interval of two years between each birth would seem to be indispensable.

It is easy to understand how the environment leaves its mark on every new creature which has grown up in it and has drawn its life from it, how ordered ways, cleanliness, family discipline, the love which comes to birth between beings, and a combination of complex, obscure, and scarcely conscious sentiments create that unique atmosphere in which the reflexes of a young personality are formed. A large part of a child's upbringing takes place of its own accord, and what is required especially of parents is to encourage, or anyway not to oppose, spontaneous manifestations. The newly-born child begins its education as soon as its eyes are opened, and the problem of knowing the age at which a parent should start remonstrating has really no foundation. If the work has been well begun, when the child is taking its first steps, it should be enough to forbid it to touch some object or to go to some place, in order to obtain this obedience with no great difficulty. This will only be possible if a certain ordered and disciplined way of doing things already exists. If a child has acquired the idea of what is dirty and what is clean, it will be easy to lead it on, as soon as it is able to walk, to understand what is allowed and what is not allowed. If the first ideas are lacking then it will be almost impossible to teach it to obey, and this presents so many difficulties that parents soon tend to give up the struggle, for it is clear that it will be a long time before the appeal to reason can be made. If a child has had the good fortune to live for a time under the system of what is allowed and what is not allowed, at an age when for a large number of other children everything is morally indifferent, it will almost naturally come to distinguish good from evil . . . . it will *feel* the difference, whereas the others will only *learn* it. The moral sense is not made out of science but out of affective life enlightened by knowledge.

For a period its parents are no more than things for the newly-born child, and for several years, till it is six years old or even older, they will seem to the child far less important and far less interesting, though far more to be feared, than say a little brother, a big sister, or some little neighbour in the street. But its parents do not know this and are not supposed to know it. Even when they do know it, they cannot bring themselves to believe that it is true. The stream of affection flows so strongly, the child's smile is so trusting and so pure, it is filled with such a rich interior life and with such a rich variety of mischief; its sadness and its tears excite such pity, its happiness is so radiant, that the father already looks on this child as a being like himself, on whom he bestows the life of his affections, the riches of his personality, and, though we ourselves have retained no memory of those first years, yet we imagine that the child will never forget those wonderful moments. It will forget them. All the same, the illusion that all this is already its life, its happiness or its unhappiness, is beneficial, for the new being is in fact prepared for life by the parental love and illusion; this illusion will produce the personality of the future. As we have already said, a child exists first of all in the eyes of its parents.

This communion of life and affection between parents and child is so strong that the father starts by being taken in by it, and is often weak and clumsy and naive when faced with its little sufferings and fits of temper; he very easily falls a victim to its childish artifices and its naïve attempts at deceit. The same is true of uncles and aunts, and, in spite of their experience, even of grandmothers. The mother is however in much closer touch with reality; though she is the first to enjoy the life of the eyes and the smiles of her child, she is much less moved by any sufferings it has to undergo, when these cannot be avoided, and she understands it far more exactly. The mother has to handle this little naked body, to turn it over and to wash it, she knows this lovable little monster and the limits of its emotions, its little obstinacies, and its way of stamping like some gluttonous little insect. Later on, no doubt, the child will cease to be a morally minute creature in its mother's eyes, whose preferences are less important than might be imagined, though unfortunately this transformation does not always take place. In most cases it is very important that the mother should have nursed or at least really looked after her child; only thus will she get to know the true dimensions of its troubles and reactions, acquiring an apparent indifference to sufferings which are noisy rather than serious, to be combined later with her infinite compassion. Before the child has attained the wisdom not to give to interior movements more than their true proportions, it has someone who is acquainted with these proportions and behaves in conformity with them. The upbringing of their children calls for strong behaviour on the part of mothers, a mixture of firmness and rough tenderness, in which physical cleanliness counts for more than sentiment, and in which the absolute gift of self and at the same time a certain reserve are maintained, a mixture of reason, of demands, of tenderness and self-denial, which it is impossible to analyse. And when, in the years ahead, there comes the tragic hour when everyone feels impotent before the suffering of a soul which is almost mature, and though the father keeps silent, the mother saves the situation with a few words. She is the only one who remembers that these are the same words which she used absent-mindedly, a long time ago—and yet it seems to be only yesterday—because the sponge was too cold on the neck of a baby.

CHAPTER FOUR

The Five-year-old Man

I

All psycho-analysts are agreed that the fundamental structure of the personality is completed about the age of five years. A child is still far from having reached its full intellectual development, but from then onwards it will have taken up a definite attitude towards the external world. A conscious life has really been formed within it, bringing with it a personal apprehension of things, rudimentary though this may be. From that age onwards it will find itself in conflict with its surroundings, and it has within it a complete organization which distorts its vision and understanding of the world, following certain fundamental complexes. Thenceforward all its experience, all that it learns, all its thoughts, will be conditioned by this complicated creation which makes up its young personality, and never again will the external world touch it directly: its mental and emotional life are affected by certain moulds. It will continue to change and will evolve, but all through its life there will be no difficulty in tracing, as the basis of its behaviour, the power of habits which were formed at that age, the influence of the dramas through which it lived at that time; many points of view which seem impossible to explain, many habits which refuse to be uprooted, are really compromises between the present and influences in the distant past, now driven into the background of the mind and forgotten. Bleuler has indeed said that from that age one can foresee in a child the form its life will take as an adult.

Before setting out along this road, we must mark it out carefully; in order to do this we will have to make an objective study of the different stages of development through which a child goes till it is five years old, watching this development from the outside only.

II

PERCEPTIONS. From the time of its birth a child is able to distinguish light from darkness. In its third week it begins to be interested in coloured objects, especially in the colour red. When two or three months old it is attracted by coloured and brilliant objects, it follows them with its eyes, and squints less frequently. It can distinguish things clearly at a distance of three yards, at five months it can see up to ten or fifteen metres, and from the time when it is one year old, it adjusts its vision to infinity like an adult. If an infant is placed near a window through which there comes a bright light, and its cot is left for an indefinite time pointing in the same direction, by continually turning its head the same way, it will end by having a certain deformation of the skull; this is specially the case with certain children who have soft bones.

As regards hearing, it is established that from the second week a child recognizes familiar noises; when a month old it can clearly distinguish the human voice. At six months it experiences pleasure when hearing music and in creating noises itself. At ten months it will sway from side to side following a rhythm which it hears. From the age of one month a child will turn alternately towards the light and towards a sound.

Its perceptions through touch also appear at an early age and develop in close relation with the other senses and in particular with the organization of the powers of motion. The formless movements with which it begins become organized fairly rapidly and, from the time when it is five months old, the child can, with difficulty, seize hold of something, with which it amuses itself. When it is seven months old these movements have become so perfect that from then onwards it seizes what it wants without having to worry about how it achieves this, for its movements have by now become completely automatic.

Its movements indeed become automatic very rapidly. When it is eight or nine months old it can sit down, and between the age of twelve or thirteen months it takes its first steps on foot. It is still ataxic. When it is two years old, it can run, jump, climb onto chairs and go down stairs, and about the age of three years, it can jump on both legs at once. From that time onwards all its functions have become automatic, that is to say it can make use of them without supervising them, being thus exactly like an adult.

The emotions are in existence from the start. In a child they accompany a number of organic changes which the brain gradually gets in check. From the first moments of life pleasure and displeasure are plainly to be observed. When about a month old, pleasure shows itself clearly in the expression of the face and is usually even accompanied by a special little cry. Displeasure reveals itself by different cries and, from the age of three months, a child has a complete pantomime by which it expresses what is upsetting it. Desire appears at the second or third time it is placed at the breast. At five months, a child stretches its arm out towards the objects it desires. Fear comes very early, especially in regard to loud noises and anything which gives a jolt. Later on, it can be occasioned by sight.

Anger only appears, briefly and intensely, after the second month. In the usual course of events it will be progressively repressed by the family. In certain cases temper will produce real emotional crises which must be treated with care.

Mental pain comes later still and is the result of an unsatisfied desire. It is sometimes hard to distinguish it from anger. Tears of true sorrow do not appear for six months, and smiles, as smiles, do not appear till about the second month, and laughter at about six months.

Attraction and antipathy are to be found at a very early age, from the time of the fifth month. To start with, they are closely connected with habit; but attractions and antipathies very soon come into being which are already linked with automatic actions and associations which already hold the field.

III

LANGUAGE. This starts by being no more than an involuntary cry but towards the age of two months syllables begin to be heard, especially those of the letter AH. The EH is not heard till the child is about seven or even ten months old. Certain sounds are produced but do not continue. From the time it is three months old, a child plays at making noises; between the ages of fifteen and twenty-one months it learns that sounds can be useful, and from then onwards language comes to have a social value. At that period it already knows the names of numerous objects and makes an effort to reproduce these words. All this cannot be done without making mistakes, and in order to make itself understood it eventually conforms to grown-up language; if the family accept the language of the child, it will cling to this as long as possible. It starts by only pronouncing words. When about two years old it starts using verbs. The use of the word "I" appears about six months later, unless the family have been in the way of using the third person. At three years old the words "of" and "for" are used, and after that are to be heard "with," "because," "when," "so that," and "if."

When two-and-a-half years old, a child knows at least 500 to 600 words. At three years old, from 1,000 to 1,400, at five years from 2,200 to 2,500, at seven about 3,000. But there are certain intelligent children who know even more, and J. Brandenburg tells of a child between four and five years old which knew about 4,300 words. This child pronounced on an average 12,000 to 15,000 words, and would ask about 400 questions every day.

This gives us some idea of the tremendous mental labour which takes place in children of that age. It has been calculated that at the age of five years a child knows more than a third of the vocabulary used by those among whom it lives. At the age of about three-and-a-half, a child only draws the head of the people it wishes to represent, but at about five years the representation is in most cases complete. It can count up to ten, but usually talks of "several" and "many." It has a practical idea of numbers and notices when some element is missing, but it is not yet able to deal with figures in the abstract.

This summary account does not, strictly speaking, reach what constitutes the real core of the personality, but it is indispensable to keep these ideas in mind, if we would understand how and out of what elements this personality is formed. Adults in general, who tend to be unconcerned with the child, when they are not actually annoyed by it, take little interest in what is taking place in its mind, and imagine that its thoughts are either empty, simple, or at times positively naughty. Adults are unaware at times that their impatient outbursts, bad tempers, prejudices, preferences and whims, leave their mark on the children who experience them. The children, for their part, do not by any means regard themselves as unimportant, with the result that they react to these outbursts by constructing for themselves their own model or means of representation of the world they encounter. We shall now study the formation of this fundamental core of the personality.

IV

Everything that we can discover in a child as the external manifestation of its mental life, corresponds with some special form in its interior life. This form will be organized round two fundamental ideas, those of time and space. Now, it is precisely the organization of the things it has learnt round the idea of time and space, especially of time, which brings about the drama in the mind of a child. A child is, to begin with, essentially a creature of the affections, and it makes its entry into life under the sign of emotion, sentiment and affection. Emotion and sentiment are not thoughts but states, and in themselves represent nothing that is organized, or logical or capable of being contained in a system. This state is either pleasant or painful, and it is a question of escaping from it or of preserving it. This is precisely the reason why the desire for organization will find its way into this mind which is still so dark, but, as can be easily understood, the organization is not made for its own sake, but in order to serve the emotional life of the subject.

From the age of two years, a child which has been brought up without love or tenderness, by indifferent or constantly changing people, will already be found in certain ways to be emotionally backward.

In fact, no matter how it has been brought up, it will have had enough experience of life for the intellectual notion of time to have developed within it. After two years, a child already has an idea of the future, and to say to it "by and by" no longer constitutes a refusal. About the age of three it can localize yesterday, today and tomorrow (past, present, future), without having an exact grasp of the day. When about four or five, it begins to have an idea of what time it is, and at about the age of five it has more or less the idea of the succession of the days of the week, and suspects the existence of the seasons.

But if these ideas have developed without its having lived amidst the same faces, the same living environment, the same affectionate adaption to other beings, then they evolve for their own sake, as something that has been acquired by the mind, *and not as the framework of the continuous life of the emotions.* Restricted though it may be, this frame formed out of the rudimentary idea of the past and the future is already too large for the capacity of a child to love it or to suffer from loving. in a normal family, if a child has need of love, *the parents also need the love of their child and this pursuit of each other extends the manifestations of fondness or the manifestations of unsatisfied needs in proportion as the idea of time is developed.* This cannot be calculated but *makes itself felt. This sense of love is not innate, it is in reality the product of an unconscious appreciation which is only possible by means of continuous contact and the experience of this contact.* The child of two years old which has not been able to pursue the love of its parents, because they are not there and it has not been pursued by their love, will have remained, as regards its affections, almost at the point where it was at birth, even though the speculative powers of its mind may have already grown considerably. We have seen this in the previous chapter. This lack of balance, which can already be noticed at the age of two years, will be very noticeable

D

when it is five years old. It will seem as if these children were not capable
of needing love, as if they were not capable of loving. The fact is, they
are not incapable of it, but their need for loving has no lasting power;
even if it is intense, it is different from that of other children of that age
who are brought up in normal families. This gap between the present as
it exists in the affections and as it exists in theory can, in certain cases,
be so pronounced that by the age of five years the hiatus can no longer
be bridged.

In practice such children live in a "time" that is affectively empty, and
in consequence do not take into account that which its duration contains:
they become attached to nothing, they regret nothing, and have no
term to their lives; later on they will become socially unstable. (Children
from orphanages, etc.).

Besides those for whom time is an empty idea, there are children, some
of whom have been spoilt while others have been brought up by old
people or by strangers who are too tender-hearted, for whom there
have always been manifestations of love at hand, which have never been
lacking, but which *have never been able to produce in them the idea that
there is an organization outside them which is stronger than they are and
with which they have to reckon.* In such children the temporal and spatial
framework of mental life is formed fairly normally, but this framework
has no really firm quality; the difficulties caused by time and space are
usually eliminated by the excessive devotion of those who have charge
of them, and are too pliant to their wishes; by the time they are two or
three years old they know quite well how to make the external world
bend to their will, for to them it is merely represented by the over-loving
people who live around them. Such children do not accept the fact that
time and space are realities which they will never dominate, and we have
here the type of spoilt children who would have no activity allowed
around them except what satisfies their desires, such as the child who
will make a hateful scene just because it is not given the moon. At the
age of five, sometimes, it will no longer be evident that such a child is
really a little monster, for, in numerous cases, its tyranny will already
have assumed a form that can be accepted . . . . but its true character will
reappear later.

A child wishes to be noticed from its earliest months, and the first
sign that its egocentrism is assuming a human form is when it tries to
retain the attention of those around it, which means that at the same time
it desires their love. Later on this need of love will take on different forms,
but it will never disappear and its training consists precisely in providing

it with something different from the family circle, by which it can be loved and which it can make the object of its love.

This need of love tends to become confused with the desire to be the centre of everything and becomes quite naturally identified with the instinct for domination, as Adler has said. The instinct for domination, or the "libido," as Freud calls it, or "egotism," according to the current terminology, are slightly different aspects of the lower and more or less instinctive form, to be found at that stage of existence, of what the scholastics call the appetite for the Good, the mystics expansion towards the infinite, and Bergson the *élan vital*.[1]

Psychiatrists will themselves speak of anomalies in the manifestations of this innate disposition, which can be pronounced or even absent, and which, in these two cases will bring about a sort of split between the individual and his surroundings, known as schizothymia.

There is, however, no need for us to spend any more time on the deviations which the inordinate love of one or both of the parents, and the unstable sentiments of those surrounding the child, may have already provoked.

V

It is at the end of the second year and at the beginning of the third that there begins what Charlotte Buhler, with an incorrect but nevertheless highly suggestive term, calls the first puberty, that is the child's first organized revolt against its surroundings, the first definite attempt to dominate or to set itself free.

John is a very good little boy, and is about to have this third birthday. He has started speaking very early, and has a fairly rich vocabulary. He has two sisters older than himself who have spoiled him a good deal, though his parents were strict enough. His sisters looked on John as an amusing doll; now, however, when he has grown bigger, he wishes to prevent them amusing themselves together, and to deprive them of every activity of which he is not the centre, while they have tended to leave him alone a bit and no longer try and satisfy his whims. He naturally plays with dolls and his sisters have plenty of these, and they specially have a number of little Japanese celluloid dolls with which they have played at taking charge of a class and at bringing up children. John sometimes amuses himself with these dolls. One evening, without any

---

[1] The English for this would, I suppose, be vital impulse, but I think most philosophers use the French term. Trs.

apparent reason, he amuses himself by killing the dolls, and before he is discovered, more than ten of them have been executed. He seizes hold of them carefully by the heads, which he holds between his finger and thumb, then crushes the faces, throws each one away disdainfully, and passes on to the next. He is well scolded but offers no explanation for what he has done; not only has he no regrets, but he says with a certain satisfaction: "John has killed the dolls." Those which have survived are hidden from him, and it is supposed that he wished to avenge himself on his sisters by spoiling their dolls. Nevertheless the method with which he set to work, and the absence of any visible emotion on his part do not fail to impress his parents who cannot recognize in this the good, affectionate little boy who up to then had never shown any sign of cruelty.

A few weeks later, John, who sleeps in the same room as his sisters, gaily tells his mother one morning that he intends to kill his sisters. "They are not good" (we know why).

He is going to break in their heads, with a knife. He has been nice to his sisters, has played with them as usual, but now threatens almost every day that he is going to kill them. It has become a daily subject of conversation, quite a gay subject, for he only talks of it in a joking way, but all the same the assertive way in which he speaks of it leaves no doubt of what is going on inside him. This little performance makes a deep impression on his parents, who do not agree with what Freud had to say about children. A few days later, while his father is reading a book, John approaches him quietly with a paper-knife, and in a playful way pretends to cut his father's foot. When asked what he is trying to do, he answers: "I am going to cut Daddy into pieces, and then Daddy will be dead." They pretend to attach no importance to what he says, and then the child spontaneously adds that he is going to kill everyone, including Mummy, because "everyone" is not good. This shows clearly the conflict between the child and its environment, and yet, at the time, nothing special is taking place—John is as obedient as ever; he would indeed seem to be a little less wheedling than usual. They have for some time past been trying not to oppose him directly, because, if he feels that a real attempt is being made to bend his will, he becomes unmanageable. A few days later, when his father appears to be asleep, John, armed with the paper-knife, pretends to cut his throat. His mother pretends not to see what he is doing, so as not to make things worse, and John says: "Perhaps he is dead." When his father wakes up, John says to him: "John thought that you were dead."

This time his father no longer laughs, and answers the child coldly, as if he attached no importance to what he has just said.

From then onwards, John becomes extremely friendly to his father, but there is something that is clearly affected in his friendliness, and one morning, when he gets up with the other children, while seeming to forget it, as if it were the most natural thing in the world, he fails to kiss his father. They believe, they try to believe, that it is due to forgetfulness, but in the evening he goes off to bed having been equally forgetful, while continuing to be pleasantly behaved. This period lasts for three days, during which time he has announced that he will also kill the little Jesus.

One evening, it is the evening of the third day, his father when he comes home finds the whole house in an upset, for John has shown himself in his true colours. During the whole day he has refused to obey anyone, and has been giving orders to his sisters and even to his mother. He has kicked his sisters in a brutal way—a thing that would not have been thought possible a month earlier—and has even attempted to bully his mother. He is in a very happy state, and seems to be quite collected, and goes on acting and playing as if nothing had happened. It is obvious that he has been scolded, but he takes up the same attitude as in the affair of the dolls. Certainly, as he thinks, he has found a way of escaping from family control and discipline.

Things have gone so far that at this moment a radical solution must be found, and this is a suitable occasion for doing so. His father quietly but firmly insists that John must apologize to his mother and sisters and ask them to forgive him, but while displaying no open revolt, the child takes up such a passive and sufficiently unconcerned attitude that his parents realize that nothing will be achieved by diplomatic means or by verbal threats. Without getting angry his father goes out and prepares a little switch, capable of stinging his calves, but too supple to inflict any injury. When he sees him come back John tries to make a desperate escape but is immediately caught. A little punishment immediately takes place, which has its dramatic side, for the child begins by raging.

The child wonders for quite a time whether he will achieve anything, but his father continues, knowing that he cannot cause much pain and can do no harm. At last, after a regular "action," the child runs away to his mother and asks for her forgiveness, after which he embraces his sisters. No grudge is borne and John, a few moments later, comes on his own account to embrace his father. A little later on, he begins to play. Before the evening is over, the child, having recovered the loving affection of his own people, seems also to have recovered his happiness. In the evening, he spontaneously embraces everyone before he goes to bed, and on the following day he is once again the good little boy. He has naturally not been humiliated on account of his defeat; on the contrary, everyone has immediately forgotten all about it.

A few weeks later, John brings a switch back to the house and says to his mother when talking about his sisters: "This is for them when they are not good." But when his father comes home in the evening, and his mother has told him what has happened, John first answers him as if he did not know what it was all about, and ends by declaring that the little switch is for when "little children are not good." He had, however, told the maid that it was for when "Papa is not good." After a few months, he starts talking once more of cutting off the heads of his sisters, and then ceases speaking of killing his near relations. At this time he has become extremely loving in his behaviour towards his father, and imitates him in everything. It has never more been necessary to use the little switch. He tells stories of how he has killed lions and bears, but in reality he is very gentle with animals and treats them as equals and regards them as his equals. He is nearly five years old and is not yet convinced that Jesus sees everything, even in the dark. He is much concerned to find a way of escaping from thus being seen, for he recognizes that the glance of Jesus not only has authority, but even has a kind of commanding force.

The conflict with his father has been to a certain extent transformed, though it is still present: it has taken the form of imitation, and indeed it ought to be so. Since his adventure when he was three years old John's life has been very rich; we have naturally not been able to give all the details here.

Finally, we must point out, before we go on to discuss this statement, that John is really a good child; he is more or less of a liar, as are most children, but very fair, distributing his sweets and kisses fairly, still an egotist, scandalized at the disobedience of anyone else, not stealing, even very little things, not greedy and without any sexual obsession, with a very great loyalty, making allowance for the inevitable little hindrances, and he is very rigid as to what can and what cannot be done.

VI

We may be astonished that the child was allowed to express such unsatisfactory ideas without being scolded on the very first occasion.

We must, however, admit that the important thing is, not that a child should not express some such ideas, but that it should not have them at all. If it is punished for having spoken in a certain way, the child will talk like that no more but will go on thinking in the same way. A child's sincerity is only possible if the parents make it possible. In this particular case, we know that the stage of wishing for the death of brothers and sisters and parents is in a certain way normal, and, if a child is allowed to express itself, it will say what it thinks. On the other hand, when a child says it is going to kill, in its mind this means "get rid of." A child of that age cannot know what death is: it scarcely has any idea of the future. Let us suppose that the parents, after the first "threat," take a tragic view of things—their child will then be for ever deprived of all chance of sincerity, driven back into its own thoughts, but without knowing the reason why. That is the time when the sentiment of hostility towards its environment will develop. We should also point out that in many families such language in a child would be looked upon as a crime, and it would be considered necessary to punish severely the language alone, when it is really only a form of sincerity, and the expression of a mind that is still in a simple stage.

If, however, this complex is not recognized, and if a series of punishments follows the acts of sincerity which the adults hold to be faults, while the child is unable to understand where the fault lies, then, rather than capitulate, anyway in its chief manifestations, *it will develop in the interior of its own soul and there it will carry out its own formation.* In a year or two hatred will be installed in the heart of this child, in the form of resentment, and this will not only be resentment against its father, *but it will be the habit of resentment.*

When a child five years old secretly bears a sort of continuous revolt against its father or against any other member of its family, what develops in it *is a way of acting, a special outlook on life which is capable of changing its object.* Its attitude towards other people and towards society in general will depend on its attitude towards its father.

When a child is not allowed to say what it has in mind, it is then obliged to hold back certain states of its soul, and this holding back, far from destroying them, encourages it to reduce them to a system. It is therefore of the utmost importance to allow children to speak with absolute sincerity as long as it expresses their genuine states of soul. A child of from three to five years old must not be driven into dissimulation by its own parents.

It seems to us that John's father did not come out of the affair badly.

He attached no importance to what the child was saying, and paid no attention to the allegorical words and gestures of which the child was unable to understand the real sense. He did not force him to come and embrace him, when the gesture would no longer have been spontaneous. But, when he had the chance to make him understand the power of the external world of which he knew nothing up to then, he made use of the blows which the child had given to his sisters—and in this case John clearly knew he had done wrong—in order to restore the principle of authority and obedience in a way that left no room for doubt. He was not scolded because he spoke of killiing, but he had to ask for pardon because he had been striking other people and this was put to him in such a way that, as a result, John learnt that the plan of getting rid of his father could not be entertained seriously. This conflict, which was resolved in a few days before any unpleasant suspicions could arise in the child's subconscious mind, brought it back once more to the state in which the desire for love was stronger than the desire to dominate, and these sentiments, having for a moment suffered eclipse, but never having been destroyed, reappeared immediately after the little dramatic scene. In such a case a child must be left to the joy of having recovered its interior peace, and not be disturbed by humiliations or further remonstrances.

The evolution of the case has shown in other ways that the method was a good one; the child has remained sincere, when expressing those states of its conscience which it believes to be lawful—and, without any exterior restraint, has never ceased to show its father every mark of love and sympathy.

This favourable evolution was, however, only possible through the collaboration of the mother, as we shall see.

It must also be admitted, as John's parents eventually recognized, they were also at fault in the explosion which took place. The fact was that they had not known what was the element to which John was specially sensitive and this little drama was necessary before they became aware of it. John came after two girls who could be made to obey without difficulty. Some little symbolic gesture had always been enough to make the eldest obey; the younger always gave way fairly easily, though it took her much longer to agree to obedience. The parents had thought they could follow the same method with John, that they could force him to obey. This did not work, and the state of general revolt to which he eventually came was to a certain extent due to his parents. Later on, they noticed that it was enough to say something to John once and then to behave as if it was certain he would do it. Obedience clearly did not always follow immediately, but for as long as the child had not obeyed all marks of affection were withheld; they limited themselves to being polite without giving him any spontaneous love or kindness. After a few hours the child would begin to cry and would decide to act of its own free will, doing so with passion as if it wished to make reparation.

It is not difficult to see that all cases are not so fortunate as this one, and that it is often difficult to avoid the formation, when the child is about three years old, of the first serious split between the child and its parents; we may go further and say between the child and its environment. The sad thing is that in most families the parents have no suspicion of this, and the child's behaviour, which they are unable to understand, only leads to reprimands which often seem to it unjust, and thus only aggravate the situation.

Everything becomes complicated when a child has not been able to find an outlet in words. In all cases when its attempts to liberate itself from its father have to be checked, the conflict takes on a benumbed character and, by an unreasoning process of adaptation, the child finds or at least looks for an ally in its environment. This is where verbal language and powers of imitation prove useful to it. The child who is suffering from such a state of discord will seek for compensation and will often find it among its brothers and sisters, and even more often in one of its parents. It frequently happens that a son takes refuge with his mother and a daughter with her father. This is the precise moment when all the special fondnesses of the parents, the secret acts of self-satisfaction which they allow themselves in regard to their children, the real or latent conflicts which can set them in opposition to each other, and which can even make their way into the personalities of their children, are going to play a primary part. A boy will start trying to wheedle his mother, and if the latter wishes to find some compensation or other in this maternal or filial love, she will without knowing it enter into the child's game, while the child is unconscious of what it is doing. The gap widens between father and son and the child soon has two ways of behaviour towards its parents, while, on their side, the parents drift far apart, sometimes without being aware of this, on the question of how to bring up their child. There is no way out from this situation, for the coldness between father and son leads to a larger coldness, in the same way that the exaggerated tenderness of the mother leads to a serious partiality, and even, in certain cases, to a defence of the son by the mother against the father, and all this takes place without anyone saying anything about it or even having thought about it lucidly. We have here what Freud has called an Oedipus complex, and it is easy to understand that once such a complex has been established and perhaps to a certain extent cultivated, the whole upbringing will become warped.

One cannot therefore too strongly recommend to fathers and mothers that they should not give way to their children's wheedling. If such a complex should seem to be establishing itself, then it is for the parents to reduce it little by little through a real collaboration, doing away with everything on which it might feed. We should observe that it is never possible to prevent the existence of such a conflict; not only is it normal, but it is necessary. It is, however, possible to behave so that it does not produce affective deviations and insoluble complexes. Thanks to this first conflict, the father and the mother, by collaborating, can transform the energy of revolt into a source of true formation.

VII

The conflict between parents and children which appears for the first time round about the third year, is in fact no more than a conflict between the principle of pleasure (the will and the whims of the child) and the principle of reality (the need for a certain standard of behaviour imposed by external forces). At that age, it is clear, the principle of reality is incarnate in the parents. In a perfectly natural way a child endeavours to escape from reality, to escape from real discipline. This effort brings about a conflict which will be either open or concealed and will only be of value to the child's upbringing if the parents are aware of what is going on. In order to escape from reality the child will take to wheedling, will make a play of affection, and indulge in pretence (this is really an adult word, and scarcely applies to a child, and in this case we would only mean the tendency to make an external show of sentiments or emotions which are really experienced but little) and unfortunately, in many cases, it will be able by these means to escape from the requirements of obedience. It is of supreme importance that each time a punishment is decreed, it should be carried out. If one or other member of the family, whether openly or secretly, nullifies the sentence, the child will know, *ipso facto, that nothing unpleasant is likely to take place as the result of disobedience, and it will make full use of this knowledge.*

And what will the child think if someone comes along who finds fault with the father or the mother, and sometimes reproaches them for not loving their child? An attitude and words of this kind are not for-gotten by it, and will give support to its interior resistance to its father or mother, as they represent and exercise authority.

It is, on the other hand, the age when, without entirely neglecting external acts and the whole mimicry of the emotions which takes place, and without neglecting verbal language, importance must only be attached to acts about which there can be no doubt. When a child's mimicry and words contradict its acts, only its acts should be taken into consideration.

However little a child is predisposed by heredity to react in a certain way, the change in balance produced by its parents' lack of sufficient care and generally unfortunate behaviour will determine this reaction for the future.

If it has been allowed to develop in this unsatisfactory way, what will the child of five years old have become like? The principle of authority, the father (we here give the word father a symbolic sense, and by it could also mean the mother or some other relation) cannot fail to be something annoying from which it will desire to escape. The way is easy enough: to pretend to give way but instead of submitting to put on a suitable act, tears, wheedling and complaints. By then fundamental habits of deceit have been installed, and thoroughly installed—and even if later conditions are of the most favourable, they will never altogether disappear. Such a child will, later on, only rarely believe in the word duty.

It will be understood that in these first attempts at upbringing there are few cases which are really bad and few which are completely good. During most of the time the parents have done as well as they could, and the result in the child has meant a mixture of unequal and contradic-tory dispositions, between them making up a fragile and sensitive personality. It is in the light of what you have just read that we should understand the effect that a conflict with its mother or father can produce in the child's mind by witnessing displays of intimate affection between its parents. Such a sight can really irritate the complex and make the child's resentment yet more deep-rooted.

It is clear that the inadequacy of parents to train their children does not cease when these have passed beyond their particularly sensitive stages.

On the other hand, as you read this, it would be quite easy to imagine that these ills were solely due to the fact that the child is brought up in a family, and that the latter is responsible for these deviations—and it is, in fact, quite clear that the family is responsible.

The family is, however, only responsible for not having been equal to its work. We ought to take it as normal, necessary, absolutely indispensable for the formation of the moral sense and social stability, that a conflict should arise in the family round about the child's third year. It is no less necessary that this conflict should be carefully controlled, that the parents should be fully aware of what is taking place, that they should be intelligent enough to see and to understand, and sufficiently well-balanced not to give way to morbid attachments or to show any signs of disturbance.

If the children follow each other too rapidly or are brought up by overworked fathers and mothers, there can be no question of any real supervision and direction. When the intelligence or the education of the parents leaves much to be desired, as well as their manner of life, good results are scarcely to be expected. We are, in short, faced at this point with bad environments, those which are of poor quality and those which are definitely vicious; to the poor quality environments should be added those of a smart and amoral type, in which there is no interest in children.

This first conflict will leave a mark on the soul of the child which will continue all through life; we have seen that it is not just the whim of a day, but a stage in its development, belonging to a period in its life. The mark left will be according to the solution which is found. These solutions vary from a dull exasperation, a permanent state of thwarted animosity, to the acceptance and love of the authority personified in the father and the mother. A happy solution is only possible if the parents at that age already recognize the independence of the child, its personal development and its value as a human being. There is one thing which the parents must constantly have in mind, the training of their child with a view to its liberty, to its emancipation, to its voluntary acceptance of reality; they must love it sufficiently to serve it, this word being understood in the sense of devoting themselves to a task. If on the one hand all this shows us the serious harm which parents can do to their children if they neglect them, on the other, when we view the question as a whole we can see the aberrations to which the military regime adopted by some parents can lead. A child is affectionate, its greatest need is that of loving-kindness, and the principle of a military bringing-up devoid of this quality which thrives in some families, goes against nature. A child brought up in this way runs the risk of being spoilt in secret by its mother or by the servants—this frequently happens—and if it really undergoes this sort of upbringing, it becomes a rebel, one who has not given his interior submission, and enters life the bearer of numerous potential sources of misfortune.

Just as discipline must be firm, when the child does wrong, so must the relationship between parents and children be based on love and affection. The two things are perfectly compatible. The punishment of a child should be short, and while it should be carried out without compromise, once finished, it should be finished. A child has no principles; everything that takes place is a form of experience from which it derives various ways of reacting. Principles will come much later, in their own time. In its early years a child must be supplied with material of good quality. If parents must be firm they must be so only in order to enable their child to love them in a pure way, without this becoming for the child a means of escaping from reality.

There is, in fact, one underlying idea at the base of the problem: the normal child, brought up in a family, has need of love. By making use of this need, by making its satisfaction subject to a certain order, parents will be able, without too much risk, to attain satisfactory results. A child which does not need love is incapable of being educated.

VIII

At an early date and in a fairly conscious way, towards the end of its second year, a child is able to dissemble certain of its thoughts, and this tendency may receive considerable encouragement from the behaviour of the family. This is certain to happen sooner or later whatever one may do, and the apparent "me" will only represent a small part of the real "me," but it is clear that the upbringing of a child must seek to reduce the opposition between appearance and reality as much as possible, and that the separation of the two should take place as late as possible and should be as slight as possible.

This separation will take place spontaneously under the pressure of circumstance. It is important that the parents should not, by imposing a theoretical pattern on a child, oblige it from its earliest days to play a part, to incarnate a being which it is not. Now it is by having trained a child very early in such a way that by the time it is two years old what is allowed and what is not allowed are two clear categories in its mind, clear though not yet complete, that the parents will have given it the best opportunity to learn how to appreciate a situation spontaneously and to express itself frankly. This should, however, never be done in a peremptory way. All will gain from the comparative calm with which the early years pass by, if the child has been trained in such a way that from the age of two onwards it can evolve freely and without constraint in the setting of its home.

A family discipline which is adapted and proportioned to the child is the *sine qua non* condition for happy development. Under cover of this discipline the fondness of the parents and mutual affection can be sustained and cultivated.

A child which is left to itself, which has not been trained, from its first steps, to respect the order around it, an order which is compatible with the life of the family, will develop by spoiling everything around it, indulging in activities innocent in themselves but which are dangerous for it, and owing to this very fact it may be reprimanded all the day long. In families where disorder reigns, where the idea reigns that children must be allowed to do whatever they like, the parents really have only one preoccupation, to prevent their children from overstepping the bounds, and giving them prohibitions. It is no use saying a child must be allowed to do what it likes! Its activity is such that if it is allowed to do so, all life becomes impossible unless disorder and dirt are to be accepted. If, on the contrary, the child bears in its mind certain elementary prohibitions and conforms to them, *it is possible for it to evolve freely, to occupy itself with its own affairs, with its games; to take trouble about them is really to indulge in what is for it a sensible activity* and to develop in peace.

In a household in which the children are brought up in so-called complete liberty, their mother's one care is to avoid being taken by surprise by her youngsters. There is no room for the children's affective life; they are only little monsters who are addressed as darling but are regarded as a calamity. If there is maternal or paternal failure from the beginning, things cannot be put right when the child is three years old; they will go on in the same way till it calms down of its own accord on reaching the age of reason. Meanwhile, a very valuable period will have been lost, with no profit to the child, indeed exactly the opposite.

In many families, when a child asks for a little brother or a little sister, it is merely told that if a little brother should arrive, it will have to give up its toys for it, and no longer be the spoilt darling of the family, etc., etc. The child would certainly of its own free will have offered its toys for the new arrival, or would anyway have shared them, but when faced with a dispossession that is at once material, for it will lose its toys, and affective, for it will lose the affection of its parents, it is obvious that it will think twice! It will indeed be fortunate if, when it is three or four years old, it does not end by saying in front of its friends: "I don't want a little brother—I would have to give up all my things . . ."

It also goes without saying that in families where the parents are always wrangling, and yield to all their emotional reflexes, and make no efforts to get over little difficulties, there can be no real upbringing for the children. Outbursts of anger, acts of impatience, and *real* slaps, will produce a primitive character in the child, with instinctive reactions. There are families in which the parents literally fight with their children, even when these are no more than four or five years old.

IX

Illness also plays an important part. When a child falls ill, its parents see it only as a loved one in danger and (this is only natural), its training then takes a secondary place. If the child is dangerously ill, above all, the love of its parents, which is powerless against the illness, shows itself in satisfying the smallest desires of the little invalid.

The result of this state of affairs is inevitable, for it would be inhuman to expect the parents to maintain any serious discipline during those difficult days; the child, when it is scarcely convalescent, will do all it can to prolong this thoroughly enjoyable situation. After convalescence, family discipline should be resumed and the sooner the better. It will be seen that the child has slipped backwards during its illness, and each time the parents will experience real difficulty in bringing it back to normal: the child has had the opportunity to discover that *a life may be possible in which the difficult efforts would be made by others,* without any great personal contribution being necessary, and it naturally tries hard to reach this happy state. At the age of even three, four or five years, and especially later, it will be exaggerating certain little symptoms feigning to have little disturbances and even to be going through little crises.

When a child is ill for several months or passes from one illness to another, as sometimes happens, no real training is possible. Such a child will suffer from the consequences later, right on till it reaches manhood. There will be unconscious egoism, a lack of will-power, a lack of inner moral sense, etc. Furthermore, it will experience greater difficulties than others in separating itself from its parental environment.

In short, the child at this time is going through the most sensitive period of its life and any upset of the family balance may have far-reaching consequences.

X

Much has been said about the sexual life of children of that age. In fact, especially during the first years, motions and manipulations of the sexual organs and an active curiosity, are often to be found; but most of the time it is not a matter of real sexual activities, and if the supervision of the parents is strict enough, these habits will easily disappear. They will tend to appear when about four or five years old, and at that time a child should be sufficiently formed to obey an order when it is given. In this way, most children will be able to reach the age of puberty without much difficulty.

We must own, however, that this sexual activity which papears round the ages of four or five years, is accompanied, especially in some environments, by a genuine sexual evolution. To realise that this is possible, it is only necessary to read the record of a court case of sexual assault.

We are not altogether convinced that genuine sexual feelings are always present. There is a certain eroticism and perhaps one might even speak of sexual pleasure; but this must not be confused with the genuine sentiment of love, as understood in the sexual sense.

It is, on the other hand, not uncommon to find, at the age of from three to five years and later, those loves of children which bind them to companions and even to grown-up people (these may even be their father or mother). These loves cannot be described as sexual, but they have an abnormal intensity, possessiveness and exclusiveness, which really monopolizes their whole affective life. The sentiment we are here considering cannot be compared with the normal forms of a child's affections; it is like a kind of sympathetic magic which in its character and intensity is very like love in the adult sense. Among healthy children, this seems to have no further consequences; there is nothing to prevent the parents behaving so as to prevent such a sentiment becoming an emotional invitation and in consequence a form of suffering too great for the childish personality. If the child's affection is centred on the father or the mother, these should be sufficiently well-informed to realize when a sentiment has become too intense, and to let it wear itself out without causing any suffering; it must above all be supplied with nothing on which it can feed or maintain itself.

From the age of three or four, sexual curiosity or at least the capacity for sexual curiosity becomes very evident. Parents should be aware of this. It is in fact on this curiosity that an elementary sense of modesty can be securely built up.

The sense of modesty must not be confused with the need of concealing the sexual organs from the eyes of other people. Training in modesty can be achieved very satisfactorily when girls can see very small boys being washed and *vice versa*, but there is something far more subtle than that. Children of the same age will not undress in front of each other after they are five or six years old, and if such precautions are normally taken from the age of four, five or six years, a child will only uncover itself in front of those who are accustomed to looking after it, with whom such a problem has never arisen. A child will itself have noticed the anatomical differences between one sex and the other at an age when this does not preoccupy it to any great extent; having noticed this it will however normally be led on to further investigations in the sexual order. These cannot fail to take place. Family life is the most favourable setting for these progressive discoveries, for it gives children the greatest number of opportunities for observing the existence of "astonishing" facts and for asking for their explanation. Parents should grade their explanations according to the age of the child.

I would insist on the fact that training in modesty does not consist in being shocked at absurd or crudely put questions, in scolding or punishing the children. On the contrary, the impression should be given that such questions are without importance, but the door should be left open to them.

But if while leaving the children every opportunity to look at what they wish (it is obvious that this does not include pornography) they are at the same time trained never to allow anyone into their rooms when they are dressing, a complete education will gradually be achieved. It would seem to us most important that the mother should very soon bring the father into the picture, so that he may be induced to respect the children's modesty. When the children begin to grow, at three, four or five years old, their father must no longer go into their bath-room or dressing-room when they are there. By protecting themselves from their father the children will learn how to protect themselves in a general way. In any case, it seems to us that the father should on no account assist at the dressing of children who have reached the age of reason, and we would consider it strange and rather morbid for a young girl of twenty to undress completely before her father, a thing which is done more often than many doctors realize.

Things must of course not be pushed too far, and a sense of modesty is not necessarily a guarantee of chastity. There are many highly im-modest people who are at the same time very prudish! While, on the other hand, there are many beings who seem to be quite lacking in modesty, but are in no sense unhealthy where sex is concerned.

We are, however, convinced that a reasonable education in modesty is indispensable. This will provide the framework within which purity of heart can be built up. Such education must begin very early; it must be reasonable, and this means that it must not become a source of anxiety for the child. Does it not seem all wrong when one sees the sisters in some country schools forbidding children six or seven years old to have bare necks or to wear short sleeves? The children naturally do not understand the meaning of this (apart from those whose sexual education has already taken place!) and they keep wondering whether they may have committed a mortal sin . . . .

Briefly, in our opinion, education in modesty should consist far more in teaching a child to behave in a certain way as regards itself and as regards other people, rather than in concealing from it its own anatomy and that of others. It goes without saying that in a normal family the children are bound to see each other as they are and that we are not speaking of adults.

On the other hand, a child has, according to its environment, varying opportunities for developing in this way. Most doctors leave the numerous advertisements which they receive every day lying about in their houses, with every possibility that the children will look at them. This method is considered by many of them to be a good one, and, when all is said and done, it may be excellent . . . .

It is only when they have grown much older that these children will suddenly begin to understand what they see. Meanwhile, their way of see-ing things and their curiosity will already have undergone an adaptation.

Children who when young have turned over the pages of the *Illustra-tion* (a relatively harmless journal) will not find in this the occasion for any sudden conscience crisis. An adolescent, however, who knows absolutely nothing, who is in a state of mental disturbance and agitation, if he should stumble on a copy of some art review, will feel he is committing a mortal sin. . . . .

You cannot prevent life taking its course; every effort should be made to prepare children so that they may meet with as few surprises as possible.

In well-cared-for families, intelligent mothers succeed in training their children in modesty, and in this they are aided by the suppleness of their minds and their intuitive powers. The troubles come from without and often enough are the result of good intentions. . . .

XI

The Adler school ascribe great importance to the inferiority complex. It is not necessary to accept the theory of the instinct for domination, of the "will for power," to admit the enormous part played by inferiority complex in the formation of certain personalities and in human behaviour in general.

It can all too often be said that education is restricted to impressing on a child the things it is not able to do. A child is, if one may so express it, being constantly snubbed by adults, whether by its parents or its elders. It is such a widespread phenomenon that it is impossible to imagine a form of bringing-up which could be completely proof against such an attitude, and, as long as it is kept within certain bounds, we consider it as a natural and normal fact which a child must face.

A child does not admit that it is really inferior and powerless, or anyway only admits it superficially, and it is constantly overcoming itself, in reaction to the conscious or unconscious challenges which the life of the adults around it is constantly making. Nor do we believe, with Madame Montessori, that this defiance of adults is likely to have a bad effect on the abilities and strength of a child. When a normal child has noticed that its ability, its strength or its tenacity are held in doubt, it will overcome all this in order to convince itself or to convince others of what it is capable of doing. It is well known that children who are only allowed pencils and who are not allowed to use ink, because they are not big enough, will seize the first opportunity to establish the fact that they can handle a pen as well as the grown-ups. This little victory, as seen by a child, is of great importance, and it is by achieving a series of little victories of this kind, in reaction against the doubts cast by adults, that a child is formed.

We can understand how harmful the actions of certain adults or certain parents may become. When a child has been so bold as to believe in itself, and has overcome one or the other difficulty which it was thought incapable of overcoming, its triumph must be accepted, and attempts must not be made to prove to it that in spite of everything it counts for nothing. If a five-year-old child produces things which are very good for a child of its age, it would be wrong to stress the defects in its work, but, on the contrary, we should share its joy and pride in creation. In all this, proportion must no doubt be observed.

The sense of inferiority is bred when real mockery, with unkind or humiliating comparisons, begins. Certain parents are guilty of this, under the pretext of developing self-esteem. If a child is constantly and with a certain obstinacy reminded of its incapacity, it will end by secretly asking itself whether it is not incapable by comparison with others, or else it liberates itself by seeking for approval elsewhere. It will very often do both things at the same time. The parents have no idea of all this, until one day, without understanding why, they will observe that the child is seeking for its standards from people other than those who are there to provide them.

Many filial or family hatreds begin thus, perhaps over a drawing or over some childish act. Indeed, this may not be their actual origin, but rather the pre-existing elements harden and get organised on such occasions.

It is in small things of this kind that the temperament of the parents already reveals itself and, later on, their faults and the temperament of the child. Some parents will be impossible to please and even merciless when shown the little creative attempts of the child, and, in proportion as their attitude differs from the average type, this will make its impress on the personality of the child. On the other hand, in proportion as a child is too sensitive in its affections, or, on the other hand, seems to be lacking in the capacity for affection, it will be too sensitive or else not sensitive enough to its environment, and will be exaggeratedly or else insufficiently affected by normal family influences. It is obvious that an inferiority complex will more frequently be found in over-sensitive children.

In a general way, its upbringing will not take away a child's hope and cannot be considered really to make it doubt its own value. Later on, when the principle of reality will have a more considerable effect, it will have an exact appreciation of itself and it is only then that the true inferiority complexes will appear, but a child must not be allowed to form the conviction that certain things are beyond its reach, before it has been able to test this for itself. The limitations of its personality should not be imposed on it from without, but the child should find these out for itself. These limitations must be discovered but the child should not lie down under them. The history of Tom Thumb's little pebbles is a good example of that process of compensation which takes place in a child where it is faced with the small amount of importance granted to it by adults. If all the children in the world for ever take us back to this legend, this is not just because it is charming, but because it tells the story of each one, for it is their normal history. The harm, in their education, would begin if, after the story of the little pebbles, Tom Thumb had in spite of this been humiliated, or punished or even not been rescued; and we can see here that a sense of inferiority easily becomes a sense of unjust treatment. It is this almost inevitable association which makes some unfortunate points of view in bringing up children so particularly disastrous.

We come across the child which is laughed at because it has some physical defect, because it fails to blow its nose, etc. It is laughed at on every occasion, in front of everybody, without taking its childish sensitiveness into account, under the pretext of correcting it, while it is incapable of doing anything in the matter and cannot correct itself. We also know the case of the child which forgets itself in bed and which is publicly humiliated, so that this may not happen again, whereas it is unable to make any change.

This unjust attitude may be due to brothers and sisters, half-brothers and half-sisters, step-parents, whether father or mother, etc. In certain cases, it is not a matter of words or gestures, but of real facts; a child really is not well treated, it is unjustly punished or it is enslaved to others. Now, we may be sure, no human being will accept a situation which it clearly perceives is an inferior one, and its mental life will so organize itself that it may suffer the less; it will turn towards some organization which rejects the established order, some refractory organization, an attitude which is socially to be regretted.

Children who are thus positively made unhappy are no doubt rare, but their situation should be stressed, because in a large number of families, owing to someone's fault, there is some child which *believes* it is the object of contempt or else unjustly treated; whether this be reality or illusion, the result remains the same. If someone secretly supports a child and, under some pretext or other makes use of the scoldings or punishments which it has had, to prove that it is not loved or that it is being unjustly treated, it will thus develop a mental attitude of reaction against its environment. The very source of its upbringing becomes dried up, if not completely tainted. The less gifted the child, the greater will be the importance of this.

Disregarding for the moment the long-range results of this inferiority complex and sense of injustice, we shall find that the most noticeable and the most certain result is that a child treated in this way will rapidly escape from the influence of its environment, by means of an unconscious adaptation and transformation, which are however adequate for this purpose, thus evolving on its own, and having no sufficient link with its surroundings, so that for this very reason it will evolve in the wrong way. The child's response to an unsatisfactory environment is sometimes mistaken for its character.

Parents must therefore from the earliest days take every precaution to be as just as possible with their children, to insist on their children being loving towards each other, and to avoid with the most complete rigour any sort of favouritism.

They must take the utmost care that no ideas likely to have serious results should be allowed to fall into a child's mind, such as: "You are just like your Uncle Z . . . . he was always the stupidest of the family," and other remarks of the same sort which should have been left unsaid. Statements of this kind can have disastrous results, for even if a child never mentions them, it never forgets them and the time will come when the underlying idea will have its effect on him. Everything which takes away a child's confidence in itself, everything which may lead it to suspect that it is not appreciated or understood by its family, tends to estrange it and to estrange it for good and all, organizing within it compensating complexes, of which the most unexpected and the most frequent will be at some time or other an utterly impatient attitude towards the smallest observation made by the members of its family—or even by strangers—and as complete indifference to what people think of it.

There are some forms of childish disobedience and of revolt which are not really either, but become for the child its sole means of survival. There is no doubt that there is no hope of curing them.

There is to be found, on the other hand, the exact opposite of these inferiority complexes, the superiority complex, based on perpetual adoration and ecstasy on the part of the parents. Such a child has no reason to train itself nor to win a place for itself. The result can be foreseen:

obedience is impossible, there is no need to win the approval of others, no need indeed for the approval of any environment whatever.

In certain families a child may be given an inferiority complex by one of its parents and a superiority complex by the other. It adapts itself to this after a fashion, and later on enters life doubly destined to misfortune, for, far from neutralizing each other, these complexes join forces, evolving on parallel lines, and making it very unlikely that the faintest moral ideas will ever form. There are thus to be found in normal and reputable circles monstrous men who do not know themselves but who are, unfortunately, known by other people!

We have done no more than draw attention to the problem, and those who would like to go more deeply into these questions will find them dealt with in more specialized works.

But, in that art which is at once so simple and so difficult, that of bringing up a child, nothing should be based on rigid rules; everything, on the contrary, depends on appreciation, on tact, on the judgment of the affections as well as of the intellect.

XII

If we have emphasized certain major errors which can be made in bringing up a child, from its earliest years, causing mental deformities, which will prove very difficult to correct, we should nevertheless point out that in all moral education, the traces of all these faults are to be found. These traces are inevitable. We have seen the conflict between the child and parent, the mechanism of what is known as the Oedipus complex, superiority and inferiority complexes, and the complex brought about by injustice. By force of circumstances, and human nature being what it is, this is to be found, in greater or lesser degree, in all evolution. Speaking of the question of injustice alone, how can we imagine any upbringing in which the child will not, at some moment or other, have the idea that it is being treated unjustly: the parents can see much further, and thus they take a different view of the situation. The essential thing is to bring about a combination so that, when a child has the impression that it is suffering unjust treatment, this impression should soon be destroyed by some mark of affection. The child must be able to love and to believe itself loved, even if, in fact or from its own point of view, people treat it more or less unjustly. This attitude, which at first sight may appear to be illogical, is really easy to put into practice.

Parents who admire a child which, from the age of five years, does not allow itself to be "downtrodden," are unaware that, from that moment, their child no longer loves them. They are unaware that, by the force of circumstances, they are, in the mind of their offspring, constantly unjust towards it, by the very fact that they are in charge of its upbringing. If the child acts openly now and then, when it can, because it feels that it is being "downtrodden," it also reacts in the same way, though invisibly, to whatever they do. If it is necessary to be very just to a child, it is also necessary to make sure that it can put up with a real or imaginary injustice without resentment.

If parents do not understand that being just is not a matter of revolting against injustice, an elementary reflex to be found in most animals and particularly in monkeys, but that it means above all that no offence must be committed against justice, then it is clear that they will not be able to bring up their children differently.

A child which cannot love someone at whose hands it occasionally suffers, will go through life under the sign of resentment; in reaction to the injustice which it undergoes, it will always be in an attitude of defence . . . . Defence! That will be its first reaction, its first attitude, when the day comes to go to school.

A child, on the other hand, whose love the parents have really been able to win—instead of merely teasing it with a lot of superficial wheedling —will be capable of liking other worlds besides that of its parents and will also be capable of needing them.

We can thus see that it is with a very complex mental organization, with very varied modes of reacting, that the man of five years old comes into contact with the world.

XIII

More than one reader may be astonished that up to now we have spent no time on the religious development of a child. The one pre-occupation of many parents is to teach their children, even when they are very young, as many prayers as possible: most of these even imagine that this premature religious instruction is all the training that is needed. If this were so, the bringing up of children would be a simple matter.

No special virtue must, in fact, be expected, because a child acquires a few rudiments of the religious life. These rudiments are necessary, but it is not till later that they will reach a real development, and will play their part in the view of the world which the schoolboy, the adolescent and the man will form for themselves. We believe that Hell should not be spoken of to children under five years old, and that this fear of punishment is in no way necessary in the training of a young child. Hell is not necessary in order to give it a fright.

As soon as it can speak, however, a child should say a very short special prayer to the little Jesus. It should have a crucifix fairly near its bed, which it should get to know, and at the same time one or two pictures of Christ (the Child Jesus, Christ in the Gospels).

A child should learn that it is Jesus who provides all good things; this can be made quite clear and easy to understand, as in the case of Santa Claus. A child will of its own accord ask a great many questions as to the part played by the little Jesus, for it is He whom it knows best of all, and it is for the parents to reply constantly and in such a way that their child may learn that there exists a world over which neither they nor it can have any influence, a world dependant on a will which nobody can reach. These are the useful rudiments by means of which a child can come to understand the world of right and wrong. Its parents must have a very clear idea that a child will only take the question of right and wrong seriously in so far as they have, during the early years, impressed on it the part played by the eye which sees everything and understands everything, the part played by steadfast justice and un-bounded love.

For, at the age of five years, religious sentiments will be above all of a magical nature, or even may already have become utilitarian, without any moral value of their own. A child attributes to the divinity all sorts of intentions and powers, and at that age there are many children who will not go to sleep unless they have a crucifix by them. We must make no mistake about this, it is not love but the equivalent of superstition, which must indeed be treated with respect because it contains in itself some useful germs, but must not be taken for anything more than an elementary sentiment. However intense the sentiment of respect or fear for religious things may be in certain children at that time, this respect or fear will be greatly affected by the direction given to the moral forma-tion of the child. If a child succeeds in taking in its parents with its external behaviour, and in giving them the impression that it is better than it really is, the same attitude will reveal itself where religion is concerned.

Here, more than anywhere else, is it possible to replace real sentiment by deceptive displays of feeling, and religion can be used by virtue of family or social language, much more easily than might be imagined. Most religious acts can be used by certain children and are used by certain adults as a simple social language with no real interior content. It is therefore highly important that in the domain of religion most of what is done should be closely connected with definite actions, expressing some undeniable gesture of the inner personality, such as sharing out sweets fairly, or saying a Hail Mary well. This latter is clearly praiseworthy, but will count for nothing compared with some little theft from a member of the family, a refusal to share sweets or a refusal to obey.

Furthermore, the depth of the religious sentiments in certain children, in their displays of feeling towards the Divinity, should not be exaggerated; for, if a child's faith in God really is something candid and simple, if it reveals itself as a touching attitude, we must not forget that at that age a child is going through a period of magic. Nothing astonishes it, and if it sets no limits to the power of God, nor does it set any limits to that of the adults, for whom it still believes all things to be possible; it even sets no limits to its own power.

A child tries to stop the rain by making signs, it makes every effort to modify external things to suit its own desires, and if, owing to some coincidence, such proceedings are followed by a result, it at once ascribes to them some all-powerful value. How many five- or six-year-old children do not imagine they are able to change the prevalent weather, by carrying out certain gestures which they believe to be endowed with power. This is a stage through which a child must pass before it realizes one day, round about the age of seven or eight years, (and it will do this inexorably), that there can be no effect without a proportionate cause. If it has not been through the magical stage, it will never reach more than a feeble idea of the principle of causality.

In short, the religious manifestations of a young child will usually express very little of its moral personality, but will have above all a close connection with its childish mentality.

For many parents, unfortunately, religion is only a social language, a way of reconciling oneself with God and with men, it is a language of rights, detached from the deeper side of the personality, which however, not only holds back, but also uses this language for its own ends. The word hypocrisy is well used in such cases, and it goes without saying that any religious training which is passed on by parents to children under such conditions, will count for nothing.

We know that a child is a natural collector and that, as soon as it is able to walk, it starts to pick up and to keep everything that it can find.

It will soon have made little collections, fruits, pebbles, insects—it collects for the sake of collecting.

Now, as it grows up, it will set out to collect the things which interest it, pieces of wood, papers, tools and nails, while girls will tend to collect dolls and pieces of stuff. There is one category among these diverse objects which will very soon be in the ascendant, and that is pieces of money.

Pieces of money are a child's real god. It attributes to them that magical power which it is indeed ready to allow to everything. It naturally does not take the value of the pieces into account, but their size and their number, and the fact of possessing these brilliant discs gives it profound happiness. It keeps them with the greatest care, asks to be allowed to sleep with them, and occupies itself with them almost the whole day long. It is a palpable god and can be used at will and it is a strange thing that even Christian parents do not hesitate to use this spontaneous deification of money, which takes place in every child (in different degrees of intensity) with a view to its moral formation. Money is the only creature outside the family that a child loves with a tyrannical love and for which it is ready to do things, not out of generosity, but out of pure self-interest. And what happens? A child is promised money if it will learn its prayers, which means that, in order to form its religious sense, it is taught—unconsciously, which makes it all the worse—to take God and religion into its service. What can be the meaning of these displays of religious feeling which really serve the secret and all-powerful cult of personal interest? The parents no doubt hope that having formed the habit of praying for reasons of self-interest, the child will continue to do so, when the reward is no longer given. The habit which will in reality have been formed is that of making use of religion, and, for most of the time, this habit will continue. How many average Christians profess their religion for any other reason than that of their material and spiritual interests? One has only to read the lists of gifts made to certain good works for the erection of some religious building. In from forty to sixty of the cases, we see that some favour is requested: a grace, a cure or some such thing, while we still do not know what the remaining donors are thinking. This means that a large number of Catholic believers never get beyond the utilitarian stage in religion, which must surely be considered as containing in itself no moral value. This has no doubt its religious sense, but such a religiosity is no different from what is to be found in many religions, if not in all, and it has none of the moral grandeur of Catholicism. If I seem to be wandering from the subject it is in order to show that the family habit of teaching religion to children by using certain attractions as a bait, is far from being a harmless one.

In many cases this first deviation is kept up at school, and all too often in Catholic schools.

The child which in the beginning used to be attracted by various objects and by pieces of money, in consequence of the evolution which it undergoes and its movement towards moral values, becomes, at one particular moment, aware of what are known as "marks." It has not necessarily lost its love of money, but, when in class, there is a tendency at work towards the idealization of these objects of value: the marks which it has won by its scholarly activity. It is still, no doubt, a case of self-interest, but it is an intellectualized form of self-interest, and on the whole this may be considered a sign of moving towards the moral life. Now, what is happening? The practice of religious exercises may bring about the earning of marks, whereas abstaining from such manifestations may lead to their loss . . . .

At five years old, moral attitudes, in their effect on the core of the personality, are very definite and arouse very exact reactions in children.

"As for me," says some little six-year-old girl, "when I am grown-up, I shall be rich. My godmother has a lot of money and when she dies that will all go to me. But I must be nice to her and always pretend that I love her a lot . . . ."

"Yes, one must be pretty sharp in this life," replies her brother, who is just a little older.

In this a product of the parental mind can be recognized.

But little Paul, who is not yet six years old and who has been discussing Santa Claus with his sisters, goes to have a talk with his parents.

"Is it not untrue that poor children do not get such lovely toys as the others from Santa Claus? Because for Santa Claus there is no difference between the rich and the poor . . . ."

CHAPTER FIVE

School

I

At the present time, the period at school is a normal part of life. There are some exceptions; in some families, parents believe themselves obliged to shield their children, or more often their child, from the influence of the school, which they hold to be harmful. If, however, we take into account what a normal person of our time should be like, to be prevented from going to school cannot be regarded as a good thing. Lessons given at home, which can only be recommended from the point of view of good instruction, are from the social point of view a very poor solution; a normal development of the affections in such conditions would from the outset require exceptional moral qualities; nor is there any cause for astonishment at the pitiful results to which such a method leads in most cases. We need not waste time on this.

Coming from its family a child, when it goes to school, enters a fresh environment. Up to now, till it was four or five years old, it has lived in an essentially closed circle, which took the place of everything else. Its formation, which was already complex, was achieved in a very close relation with this circle. The idea which it has of itself, it receives from its family; it may be a little prodigy before which everyone bowed down in admiration, perhaps it is a little tyrant, or deceitful, or unappreciated and longing for justice or affection; perhaps it is simply unable to say, like its older brothers and sisters, that it can read and write. It may be spurred on by pride or by envy, perhaps the hope of escaping from family discipline or a mysterious enthusiasm to seek adventures in an unknown world. Most of the time it can be all these things at once, with one or the other dominant according to the previous experiences of its life, according to its fundamental disposition and according to what it has heard told.

All this could be summed up in one word, by saying that the slightly anxious aspiration of a child to go to school is an act of growth which is also, although unconsciously, a gesture of liberation from its family. It is with a certain joy (for the first time in its life, one could even speak of happiness) that the child leaves for school, at least in the greater number of cases.

The entry into its class, however, and its first contacts, are also its first serious disillusionment. In most cases adaptation is a rather painful business, we could even say it takes the form of a conflict. We cannot state precisely what happens at the moment, but it is true to say it has a two-fold experience: on the one hand, it is suddenly separated from its family environment, on which, without being aware of it, it has up to then been totally dependent, even living by it morally; on the other hand, the school environment is immediately seen as a sort of order from which there is no escape, one which watches it and is indifferent at the same time, and faced with which it feels utterly powerless and utterly small. Being suddenly deprived of the picture it had formed of itself when within its family circle, it feels it must adapt itself to a far larger framework where it will count for much less. It has at the same time a sense of sadness and of perplexity; having left with much cheerfulness, it is with a disturbed little face that the new scholar returns home. In accordance with its previous upbringing and the habits of self-control which it has so far acquired, it will settle down for better or worse, and will bear what comes its way with more or less courage; but the time comes when its tears break out, and when it begs in a pitiful way: "I don't want to go to school, I want to stay at home . . ." In spite of their love, the parents must hold out firmly against this suffering; they must not give way; it is for them to win the first battle when the child has to face life, to force it to face reality, to conquer, for the first time, the desire to retire into itself, to refuse its destiny. The gate of Paradise is shut; the child, like the first man, will try to knock, will hope to hear steps coming to open it; its first five years are finished for ever. But the sun will return. When the early days are passed, and a child has accepted the fact of its being so small, other friendships will be formed, other faces will enter into its life. The competition with its father or its mother, with its brothers and sisters, loses its exclusive importance, for here are innumerable models, innumerable competitors, here there is something which may in the long run be even more interesting. Gradually, as soon as the uprooting has become less painful, a child which has gone to school will reconstruct its own life . . . .

The reactions of a child to the exigencies of school are very closely connected with the state of its personality, and the mental dispositions with which it faces them are conditioned by its previous experience of life. The influence of school will no doubt be enormous, but it can only be exercized through the medium of the ways of behaviour which have already been formed in a child by its family life. The new little scholar is not a new being; it already represents a history, a history that is unique from the beginning of time, and beneath the apparently simple appearances of the many children who come every year to join the ranks of the pupils, to which their educators can, by the force of circumstances, give no more than a welcome, and to which knowledge is presented in stereotyped form, there is given to society a multitude of beings which are something completely new in the history of the world, a multitude of beings with organisms, heredity, and past experiences that make up something so individual that there can be no question of assimilating them with each other, above all of assimilating them with the children of yesterday or with those of tomorrow.

The school will try and make this being, which cannot be changed into any other, conform to a certain type; it will succeed in making the new postulant, if it has any adaptability at all, into a being that will act in co-operation with many others, in other words, into a sociable being. It will in fact only have created two forms of being which seem to be alike; the unconquerable differences between them, which are to be found in the newly arrived pupils, will persist throughout every act of conformity in their behaviour, the same passions which are to be found in adolescents can be found without difficulty in the as yet unformed child when it arrives timidly at school. The products of going to school do not consist of the sum-total of ideas learnt, of rules of conduct accepted, of ideals dimly seen; they are what this man of five years has made of all these new things, they are the results of the programme being assimilated by the man he was when he entered the school, but which has been progressively enriched.

Life at school will always produce two results: the results which have apparently been achieved, which would seem to be common to a large number of human beings living in the same world, and the inner complexes of the personality which this life has brought about.

The teaching staff would be able to teach the twenty pupils in a class how to write twenty fairly similar essays about the love of our neighbour; but behind these twenty similar essays there will lie concealed twenty entirely different personalities, twenty entirely different conceptions of this love.

While the first years are so important that they can never be deprived of a personality all their own, the school, in preparing an individual for social life, will give a social expression to this fundamental core. Even if it is certain that these "social forms" of behaviour are no more than outward semblances, yet we must not lose sight of the fact that the intimate dispositions of a full-grown being are a compromise between what it was when it first went to school, and what the school taught it to be, and that this compromise will bear the stamp both of the child's life before it went to school and of the realities which it learnt at school. The connection between the two is a very close one, and the combination of compromises and complexes which make up a human personality at the end of its time at school, will be conditioned by the combination of events which took place during that period. The real man, when his schooling has come to an end, is as indelibly marked by his own school life as he was by his family in his early childhood. And just as his schooling was only able to enter into him and to influence him through the medium of his childish personality, in the same way the rest of his life will only affect him through what he was when he left school.

School life is made up then, it is clear, of what is taught, what is told, the opinions which are held there, and its social and moral educational climate. In the eyes of a child, everything belongs to the same category.

An essentially neutral thing, as that two and two make four, can be taught with such a number of imponderables that one has only to think of this to be aware how impossible it is for there to be any really neutral education, and to realize the immense influence a school can have on the formation of a personality, quite apart from the purely documentary side. We shall now try and see, in broad outline, the influence which the school has in the development of a child.

II

In talking of school, we must first of all know the purpose which it serves. To many people the answer will no doubt seem simple enough: the school is there to teach the greatest number of things which will be useful in life. But it is not altogether that. We must first of all remember that a child, quite apart from all questions of school and when left to itself, undergoes a certain mental development, and endeavours to satisfy certain needs which make their appearance. Thus, about the age of seven or nine years, a child will make its first efforts towards a rational understanding of the world, efforts which will reach their full activity round the age of twelve. Whether it goes to school or not, a child will form its own picture of the world. It will not be the rôle of the school to bring to birth a child's first attempts at synthesis, for it would be incapable of this, but to nourish its intelligence in such a way that these syntheses will be of the richest possible. Just as a surgeon does not create the cicatricial power of the cells, but makes use of it, in the same way an educator does not create the intellectual needs or intellectual labour of a child: he nourishes them. By bestowing on a child the power to read and write, in teaching it the use of figures, a schoolmaster enables it to enter into personal, direct contact with past and present humanity, to have a share in moral, scientific and social traditions, and at the same time in the great currents of thought of the day, as they make their way through the society of which it forms a part, and of which it could have no knowledge if it played truant.

The school, in this sense, not only instructs the child, but gives it possibilities of indefinite growth, of constant improvement. The school broadens to infinity its basis of contact with the world. A child, however, which has been suddenly plunged into such an accumulation of materials, is not able to keep abreast of them, in spite of the need it has to understand them, and will accept with much credulity the little syntheses within its reach which the master proposes to it. Catholic teaching, if well understood, should give a child a universal and eternal setting for its life. But is there such a thing as a well understood Catholic education?— The programme of the Central Council of Catholic Primary Education (1936) gives good ground for hope.

Schools of the totalitarian type will without fail narrow down as much as they can the possibilities of any development towards the universal: while teaching children the legend of the new myth, their educators will desire them to feel the need for nothing else, and will produce "anarchical" syntheses. Once, however, a man is in possession of the means of development, he will not halt, and these glittering myths are, owing to the very nature of man, destined to crumble away on their first contact with reality.

The fault which must be found with all national and totalitarian schools, must also be found with a good number of Catholic institutions, whose chief concern would seem to be to prove to the pupils that only folly and bad faith are to be found outside. With a large number this is no doubt very successful, and when a politician of the left, an atheist or a sceptic, is mentioned, there is often added:—

"Former pupil at a Catholic school . . . ."

And there are certainly those who glory in this. But does this not simply show that the school in question was not able to retain its hold on the pupil up to the completion of his intellectual and moral development?

F

We must be careful not to attribute all Catholic disillusionments in these matters to a bad spirit.

In reality, however, the evil goes very deep. We do not think there is much cause for hope; for it is not enough to have excellent secondary schools; we also need good primary schools, a good average education and so forth. This may not be the best place for tackling this problem; it is in the cultural and scientific domains that it plays the largest part.

It is not enough for us to show triumphantly that we are following in the wake of progress; the battle goes to those who create progress . . . . the strength of the resistance shown by Catholic education to new-fangled fads is often quoted. This resistance is, alas, far from being a myth!—But it also has another name.

Round about the age of seven, in fact between seven and ten years, the moral sense begins to function, leaving the child with the impression that its acts are free. No educator creates a "moral sense." This takes place of its own accord, and round about that age, however unfortunate some of the elements may have been which have gone to its formation, a child will judge certain acts and activities "morally," distinguishing between good and bad. If left to itself this "moral sense" or if preferred this "conscience," which the child has, is unlikely to prove of much value. *In the realm of conscience as in that of pure intelligence, the school will supply considerable enrichment, but can also be the cause of deviations, some small and some serious.*

Under these conditions, if the philosophic system of the school differs from that of the family, a conflict will arise. If the school is a continuation of the family, this conflict can only be solved in one way: the changes in moral attitude, apart from certain exceptions, must be an improvement of the family way, with no appreciable destruction of what is already there; not only must the school provide no occasion for justifying any doubtful attitudes, but it must urge the child onwards to ever higher attitudes in the moral hierarchy. On the other hand, if the school is completely individualist or in certain ways libertarian, a child will find the opportunity to justify a number of attitudes which, in their family circle, would have to be suppressed. And, as the need for unity is even more marked in a child than in an adult, these newly-tolerated attitudes will serve as materials in its moral evolution. The real personality of a child, as it well knows, is not exactly that which it shows on the outside, but this hidden personality desires to come to the surface and to justify itself: it is ardently set towards the world without, and every reflexion, every hesitation, every smile on the part of its masters is observed. A child of from six to ten years old, which is sensitive to every facial expression, and is extremely sensitive to every reaction, is extremely quick at capturing the atmosphere of any special environment, and whatever may be the moral teaching which is given in theory, the moral formation of a school will always conform to what the masters really profess, especially if this is easier than the moral code of the family.

Furthermore, the affection and the sympathy which unites the scholars to their masters must not be ignored, and the efforts at adaptation which a child quite naturally makes to accommodate itself to the personalities of its teachers. This affectionate relation which schoolmasters experience but often fail to notice, is very lively in children, and plays a rôle which wise educators can find very useful.

School thus directs and enriches the spontaneous intellectual and moral evolution of a child; it does not produce this evolution but it makes use of it, and it is because a school gives a decisive turn to an evolution which only takes place once, that it is such an important factor in the formation of a personality.

III

An average intelligence, when it has reached the end of its primary education, is able to communicate with other intelligences by means of the written word. This power does not provide humanity with anything new, but makes it possible to move a great number of individuals in the same direction. It establishes a cohesion between beings who are widely separated from each other, and enriches the area of contact between the individual and the collective soul, in proportion as the racial group to which it belongs is numerous. It establishes a continuity between the past and the future. The floating mass of minds whose life remains rudimentary in spite of everything, and does not rise above the level of our dailies and our films, represents a vast sea from which a few intelligences now and then emerge. A school provides the conditions which are necessary to awaken the desire for intellectual expansion, and though the majority may only pursue it unwillingly, there are those who become enamoured of the life of the mind. It allows for a process of selection among a large number of individuals, a selection which is proved to be indispensable if we think how there is only a handful of men throughout the world who are able to follow Einstein or Poincarè in their mathematical reasonings. Below them, there are a few thousand intelligences which reach a really extraordinary development, while the general run never get beyond the rule of three. There are thus only a few men who make up the spear-head of progress, but these few men are only possible because thousands and thousands of men have come into contact with the mysterious language of numbers. . . . The class they attended did not give them their genius, but it revealed a world to them, and then it made their genius fruitful, *by relieving them from having to begin again on their own the history of mathematical thought.*

When a little Sister in a convent school, in her maternal fashion, patiently and with a smile, explains to some children who have not gone to sleep and whose minds are not wandering, that bread is a wonderful thing, that it is made out of flour and that the flour is made out of grains of corn, of that corn which grows in the fields quite near them, of that corn which has to be planted, then allowed to grow, to be tended and cut and then brought back to the barn; that it then has to be threshed in order to release the grain which is then taken to the mill, that mill which can be seen down in the valley, and which is turning at this moment; when she adds that this grain will slip down gently between two large stones which grind it into a white powder, so light that it flies up into the air and which has to be carefully collected together; that this white powder which it has required so much trouble to obtain, is the flour with which their mother makes the bread: it is perhaps on that morning that the children will for the first time see bread as it really is, will experience on that occasion a sort of respect for things, a respect which will become an important element in their moral lives. Later on, most of the scholars will remain indifferent to the account of how coal was formed, of Papin's discoveries about steam, or of Stephenson's locomotive; but some of them, when they are told the story of Denys Papin, will remember how they have often watched the cover of the family saucepan rising up, without thinking about it, but finding a certain pleasure in watching it, and then will feel secretly humiliated that they did not give more thought to the matter, and will instinctively decide to improve their powers of observation, and to make up for this reverse.

Whereas a child of five, when it returns home, is quite content with making a mill with paper and string and sand, a schoolboy of ten is no longer capable of having this illusion. *The principle of reality and the rational point of view have in the meanwhile found their place in its world of thought and in order to conquer Denys Papin he needs a machine which really works.*

The history of steam naturally only plays a symbolic rôle here, and the whole history of man is at the service of a schoolboy.

A school is a true society and all the social life around it becomes transformed into activities adapted for children. Childish societies have been very closely studied by specialists in education. In school circles they have a predominant influence on the pupils. They are clearly a reflection of the mentality of the masters, but also of the family and social environment. Their essential value is that they are a powerful aid to controlling the emotional and affective life of the children. Their tears and their tempers can only last for a certain time, can only be indulged on certain occasions, and may not exceed a certain intensity. Sulks receive no response, nor does any maudlin sentimentality, and in general the environment tends to form the pupils according to the ideal of the surrounding social type. Those who are unable to conform and those with morbid temperaments, as well as thieves and cheats, receive rough treatment and sometimes are ostracized. However, as in all simple environments, the societies of school-children are indulgent and tolerant, and any ostracism only continues in exceptionally bad cases. Mockery and irony play a predominant part in applying sanctions.

Their sense of justice is strongly developed, but in the egocentric way that children have, without taking much trouble to be objective, and the life of every child at school will include some episodes when it has to submit to injustice, and which it has had to bear without any exaggerated reaction. When we reconstitute the past life of our invalids or of our delinquents, it is from that age that anomalies begin to be seen. This environment eventually frees the seven to ten-year-old child to a certain extent from its great desire to win approval: a group of school-children has no pity for the pupil who acts *solely* to please the schoolmaster, whether from fear, servility or self-interest. All this is noticed and cured in the most ruthless fashion, unless it is just a matter of a few small digressions.

In such childish surroundings the various local events, the scandals of the neighbourhood or of the village, the glorious events of the locality, and above all stories with a strain of the marvellous, play a very important part. Educators should know this, for the view which school-children have of the world is first and foremost restricted to the world of school. Thus do extraordinary powers, magical powers, stories of miracles and heavenly interventions, stories of fairies and ghosts which make up the mysterious patrimony of every community, receive from each generation of school-children a fresh impulse and power of suggesting something new, according to the fashion of the day.

It is through all this phantasmagoria, while always making the effort to adapt it to its own mentality, that a child becomes conscious of the great events which its school sets before it.

It is therefore highly important when teaching to make use the whole time of the interests which have been aroused in the child through the evolution of its own personality.

Nevertheless it sometimes happens that "centres of interests" are treated in the most absurd way: subjects are introduced which are unsuitable for a child's age, and which require a form of intelligence which it does not yet possess.

In proportion as it becomes familiar with methods of calculation, with the rules of grammar and the rudiments of science, a child's mind will become compelled to keep ever closer to reality. The gap between dreams and reality must grow progressively less, but this evolution takes place at the expense of the element of pleasure; it thus happens that at each stage of its life at school a child is held back by the imaginative elements in its character, whereas the laws of its mind are demanding, almost against its will, that it should submit to facts. A child constantly finds itself in a state of unstable balance and is tempted to look backwards more often than it should. Playing pranks, turning back towards its family, insubordination, these are all methods which can be used in order to free itself from this close contact with reality and with society. Furthermore, even when things are seen in the most favourable light, childish points of view never entirely disappear, and every man, in some compartment of his mind, has a corner reserved for childish ways.

Sport can be so engrossing that it fends off the need for submitting completely to the hard principle of reality. It is a form of escape. It is both a good and a bad thing, for it is difficult to preserve the right proportion.

Indeed, this consecration by an adult of the remains of a childishness which former generations, whatever we may say of them, kept courageously in control, when made in the form of standardized sport, constitutes a pressing problem for the future. There can be no doubt that at the present day there is in existence a vast, sustained, carefully planned movement at work, when we take into account the number of individuals who fail to come to maturity, and the possibility that they may be kept indefinitely in this condition. This is intimately linked up with the question of the moral sense, the formation of which takes place during the years at school, while it is also connected with the religious

question and the surrounding political philosophy. We shall come across
this later on. About the age of twelve years the principle of reality is
established, and a child becomes capable of full mental activity and
control.

IV

Let us rapidly go over the necessarily incomplete account which we
have just given of life at school, and we shall find that:

(1) The fact that a school should teach a child to read, to write and
to calculate is of the first importance. A school should not, however,
confine itself to endowing a child with these capacities with a view to
its using them in the future. It should use them immediately; even the
most summary rudiments should start for a child the widest possible
contact with human thought and history. It is not a question of knowing if a child understands exactly, but solely of providing it with the
materials for the mental constructions which are at work within it and
will contribute to its formation. These constructions are made spontaneously, and are never more than given a direction, and such are
the laws of the mind that the more numerous and the more significant
the materials which are procured for the child, the richer will be its
development. A primary school course at the end of which a child
would be able to read perfectly, to calculate perfectly, and to write
without a mistake, but had only learnt to do so in an automatic
fashion, by means of unmeaning phrases, without having been really
brought into contact with human history, would be a monstrous
affair, for it would atrophy all intelligence. Even if no such school
exists, we all too frequently meet with those which are very like it.
The teaching of children is all too often entrusted to individuals who
are absolutely indifferent to human culture, and this defect is frequently to be met with in free education. The resistance of one whole
part of our educational system to new conceptions can be all too
easily explained, and it is in the name of Catholic morality that one
most often hears educational innovations condemned by a lot of
pedants. Not all of these, no doubt, are very interesting, but these
inveterate primary school men seem to be unaware that no progress
can be made all at once and that there can be no progress unless one
is willing to leave the solid ground so as to feel one's way ahead, an
attempt which may well go astray.

(2) From the point of view of moral formation, going to school brings about several important results: (*a*) it makes it possible for a child to judge its family environment by comparison, whatever may be the value or advisability of such a judgment; it is in consequence necessary to foresee that the spirit of the school will extend into that of the family, broadening this more and more (family, group, hamlet, village, nation, humanity, the Catholic representation of the world being, it would appear, the most fruitful); (*b*) the obligation for the child to take its part in the society of the school, which is a true society with its own customs, its ideas about courage, fear, etc., with power to enforce conformity, a society which has an immense influence on the external behaviour of a child, notably on the creation of those reflexes which restrain the emotions and the sentiments.

There is something to be added to this: for many educators, this spontaneous organization of a certain moral outlook is a fortunate phenomenon, which must not be impeded, and is in a certain sense the experimental proof that men are of their own accord moving towards a certain moral outlook, all religious considerations thus becoming useless or even having an adverse effect on natural evolution. We may perhaps be allowed not to hold this view. It is certain that there is an organization with a certain moral outlook in children as a group. When, however, their experiences are analysed from rather closer at hand, we are forced to grant that in this case, as in that of the intelligence, there is a natural evolution, along the main lines of the human mind, but that if this is left to itself it will be of very poor, one might even say of wretched, quality. Inhibitions of emotional reflexes do not belong of themselves to the domain of morals and in this respect have no moral value.

The one great weapon of these societies is ridicule. On the other hand, the sense of justice, as far as it can be said to become developed in a child, is for most of the time only negative or neutral in form: "You mustn't have that which we haven't got and you must share it with us." This sort of justice is only a socialized product of the most complete egoism. Justice may be the result of this egoist movement, maybe, but this movement does not constitute it as justice. We have also spoken of the courage of children, of the devotion which they can show to their own people, and this is true enough, but really thought-out courage, going as far as a sacrifice which has been planned beforehand, is rare enough in societies of children, and when it is to be found, it is usually in imitation of some courageous act, which has been previously admired by the child. Now, the point we would stress is that the imitation of this courageous act is only possible if an example has been set before the child, and if thus, in consequence, an external element has come to play a part in the spontaneous evolution of the child. This external element is the idea which is set before the child that *it should identify itself with some special person*, (with Christ or with Hitler, for example) in accordance with its dispositions, both natural and acquired.

Now it is part of a child's mentality, not only that it is receptive of the stories of myths and heroes which it is told, but that its development requires that it should have such examples set before it. A child also absorbs everything of that kind that it is told with extraordinary avidity, as long as this is adapted to its mentality. Those in charge of schools can do what they like with the children, and it is at school that social types are formed. If a child does not go to school it will choose heroes from outside its normal moral environment, but it will choose them all the same.

The time at school also corresponds with the period when a child is most receptive to its relationship with things, with nature and with animals. A school usually tends to destroy this. An average pupil about twelve years old, when leaving any primary school, is for ever incapable of seeing the sun for himself, incapable of discerning the mystery in things, and its emotional side is reduced to its lowest terms.

CHAPTER SIX

The World of the Child Six Years Old

What we have just said about school represents the adult point of view. We have a way of understanding things and, without being aware of the fact, we bring human beings within its bounds. In our relations with people of our own age, we form a picture of them which we believe expresses their real personality but which is at heart no more than a symbol, and this symbol is to a large extent the product of what we are ourselves. From time to time we have cause to learn, and often enough with some amazement, how much this symbol differs from the reality. As long, however, as no special event has come to shatter the construction which we have erected by means of this rather summary picture, we do not feel that we are called on to revise or complete it.

We thus see that we understand our children through the medium of the more or less precise ideas which we have formed about them, but these ideas are without any true insight into the mental world in which the children live. It is not, however, indispensable for adults to have this insight, if we keep to the simple question of the relationship between parents and children. This evolves rapidly, conforming more and more to the adult point of view as it does so, while the use of the same language and the same grammatical forms conceals from each side the profound differences that lie beneath the same word or the same phrase. This mental world of children is not easy to get to know: at the time it differs most, round about the ages of five, six or seven years, a child is unable to express itself correctly and as its powers of thought are as yet undeveloped and it is not greatly separated from the world around it, it feels no great urge to oppose its own view of things to that of the grown-ups. It lives and evolves, and it is not aware that it is living in a kind of mist from which it is gradually emerging. Meanwhile, the parents scarcely suspect that this childish evolution is taking place; they treat children, when left to their natural inclinations, as a reduplication of themselves in miniature.

They themselves have only very indistinct memories of that marvellous period, precisely because at that time their conscious ego was not yet complete, and they are thus incapable, for that very reason, of reconstituting the stages through which they have passed. We therefore can only reconstitute this childish world by systematic study; this study is difficult and relies on hazardous constructions; it is nevertheless essential to know a few of the main lines. Moreover, there are a number of adult points of view, and many lines of argument which cannot be reduced to logic, but which nevertheless exercise a great influence on men's thought and behaviour, and can only be understood if we cast our glance backwards, to the age when this way of seeing things was habitual and all-powerful.

I

One of our friends has told us, with a certain retrospective astonishment, that when a child he had discovered a way of finding lost objects which was even better than a prayer to St. Anthony. It consisted simply, when he knew roughly whereabouts the lost object would be, of throwing another, as like to it as possible, in the same direction. They then went to look for the second object, and while looking for this they would find the first. It is easy to understand what really happened; he did not, however, see things from that angle; the fact of throwing the second object held for him a kind of mysterious power, and the proof that he believed in it is to be found in what followed. One of his sisters had lost an ear-ring in the garden, and they had searched for it in vain; even prayer to St. Anthony had been a failure. He claimed, however, little six- or seven-year-old creature as he was, that he would find it. He only asked that the second ear-ring should be entrusted to him for a few minutes. When he had it in his possession and was alone (he was aware that the grown-ups would probably look on him as foolish) he threw the second ear-ring in the direction where the first was presumed to be. It was on a lawn and the rest of the story is easy to guess; both ear-rings were lost. Our friend was well put out of countenance by the affair, and it no doubt taught him to beware of hastily formed convictions.

This little story, which will seem naïve and absurd to grown-up people, corresponded with something precise and certain in that child's mentality. Can we give it a definite place in the evolution of a personality? The studies of Jean Piaget will have something to tell us on this subject.

This attitude corresponds with a stage which Piaget calls: *Magic by participation in gestures and in things.*[1] A child carries out some mental

[1] Magie par participation des gestes et des choses.

activity or even performs some gesture and acknowledges that this exercises an influence on some event which it has either hoped for or feared. Other cases are to be found in which magic is to be found by participation in thought or in things: a child has the idea that reality can be modified by a thought or by a word or by a participation in intentions. In the latter case bodies are deemed to be living and to have intentions of their own; animism is a case in point; a child believes that the will of a body acts on that of others and the magic (the word must naturally be understood in a very broad sense) consists in making use of this participation. A child can be seen ordering the sun or the clouds to follow it. In Piaget's work, *The picture of the world in a child*,[2] will be found numerous examples of this mentality, which disappears more rapidly with some children than with others, in proportion as the powers of reasoning develop, and along with them, the understanding of physical causality as well.

One can, however, still find this type of outlook in normal children of from ten to eleven years old. Can it be said to persist in an embryonic manner in an adult and that no normal personality ever sheds it completely?

It is clear that during this period of extreme animism and magic a child is particularly receptive to all tales of wonder and that religious faith, the power which it believes supernatural beings to possess, really has only a very natural meaning in its eyes.

A good way of approaching a child's animism is to study the consciousness with which it believes things to be endowed. Piaget at this point distinguishes four stages, which do not necessarily follow each other, but which can overlap each other very closely.

In the first stage: *everything is conscious*. A child never says that everything is conscious. It merely affirms that every object can be a seat of consciousness at a given moment, that is to say, when the object is active to a certain degree or is the centre of some activity. A pebble may thus feel nothing, but if it is moved, or made wet, or broken, then it will feel this.

Here are the answers of a child about eight and a half years old, Jack.

Jack declares that only animals can feel a prick, but he shows that he can give a finer shade to his replies. The clouds, for instance, would not feel the prick. *Why?* Because they are made of air.

Do they feel the wind or not?—Yes, it pushes them along.

Do they feel the heat?—Yes.

[2]La representation du monde chez l'enfant, (Paris, Alcau, 1938).

Does the bench feel anything?—No.
Does it feel anything if it is burnt?—Yes.
Why?—Because it becomes smaller.
If I tear this button (from your jacket) does it feel it?—Yes. *Why?*—Because the thread is broken. *That will hurt it?*—No, but it will feel that it is being torn . . . .

In a second stage, consciousness is from then onwards restricted to movable things, that is to say, no longer to bodies which are, for the moment, the seat of some movement, but to those which are usually in movement, the stars, clouds, rivers, wind, vehicles and fire.

In the third stage those bodies are conscious which have a movement of their own; at this point reflection has already taken its place. The answers obtained at the first two stages show that in general the child has not really given its mind to these questions; it submits to a certain state of affairs and when questioned it gives certain replies to which it has given little thought. On the other hand, when it reaches the third stage, it is thinking clearly.

Robin is nine years and nine months old. He grants consciousness to animals but not to the table. *Would a table feel it if it were pricked?*—No. *Why?*—Because it is not a person. *Does the fire feel anything?*—No. *If water is poured over it does it feel anything?*—No. *Why?*—Because it is not a person. *Does the wind feel anything when there is some sunshine?*—Yes. *It knows that it blows?*—Yes. *Does the sun feel anything?*—Yes. *What does it feel?*—It feels that it warms.

Robin also ascribes consciousness to the stars, to the rain, to the stream, but he refuses it to bicycles, motor-cars and boats . . . .

Finally, the fourth stage restricts consciousness to animals. This stage usually appears round about the ages of eleven and twelve years. Of inanimate objects the sun usually remains endowed with consciousness the longest. The most notable characteristic of all this evolution is its fluctuating quality; it is also very slow in operation, and most children seem to feel little anxiety about the matter; in many cases it was only the examination which made them give their minds to the subject and make progress.

Those who have not taken part in these examinations will be a little surprised at how tenacious and universal this animism can be. We can remember, however, having witnessed a little scene which gave reality to one of these experiments, but in a spontaneous way. The subject was a little eight-year-old girl, who was already very good at addition and subtraction, who was studying geography and could say that there was a time when the sea covered our country, and so on . . . in fact, a regular little blue-stocking. One evening she was playing with a little toy man on a spring which was crawling about on the floor, and which, when it came up against an obstacle, would swivel round and go off in another direction. To everyone's stupefaction she asked:

"But how does it know it must turn round like that?"

In this case the child ascribed consciousness to the toy, while taking into account that its means of knowledge could not be the same as those of a living being. In order to stress that what she said had good foundation, she went on:

"But it's the same with the mouse that is able to run about on its own, but it also has to pay attention to this . . ."

But she said no more. Nothing more can be known. She probably did not have to reconcile what she had experienced with the picture which she had formed. Six years later, we spoke to her of what happened; she no longer remembered it and very much doubted that she had ever held such ideas.

Parallel with this animism there goes a tendency to ascribe intentions to things, and we shall find this attitude once more in the evolution of the moral sense.

This all has an interest which far surpasses that of simple erudition. We would consider that it is most fortunate for children that adults do not get a clear idea of the pictures which they form for themselves; if they did so one would find parents and teachers vying with each other in their attemps to cure the children of these false imaginations, and it is easy to understand what disorders could easily be formed in their mentality. In this connection we should point out that the children examined by M. Piaget had not, in most cases, received a religious education. The observations made in their cases will thus throw into full relief the spontaneity of their evolution. They also bring out the fact that this evolution will take place, even if no attention is paid to it or even if the adults do not suspect it. The question we are faced with from the point of view of religious education is this: should attempts be made to bring a child's animistic outlook to an end prematurely, with an over theological religious explanation, or rather should religious instruction be adapted to the childish mind? Our experience has been that religious instruction, if it is given in a clumsy way, with premature attempts to explain the question of the soul of things and of beasts, only succeeds incompletely in transforming the childish outlook, and indeed, it on the other hand strengthens interior objections and contradictions. These do not necessarily become explicit, but all the same they act as a substratum to points of view which will later on assert themselves more boldly, especially at the time of puberty.

II

When studied solely from the aspect of animism, a child may seem to have little solidity, to be fragile and an easy prey to all sorts of errors. But we cannot remain content with only one aspect of things. At the same time as the animistic outlook of the world evolves in a child, there also develops that collection of processes, which are analysed under the title of *La Causalité Physique chez l'Enfant*.[1]

This study is extremely arduous. Piaget distinguishes no less than seventeen different intermediary stages between the sheer animism of the start and the arrival at the idea of physical law. As it would be impossible here to take up all these questions, we will confine ourselves to giving a short account of them, and will try and make it as clear as possible.

Three periods can be distinguished in the evolution of the idea of law in a child. Each of these periods is characterized by its relationship with that which is necessary and that which is universal. During the first period, nothing exists which is universal—there is no universal law. As for necessity, this is a purely moral question. Things act or move owing to a moral and purely social obligation. There is no physical determinism. In the second period, these two types of necessity grow different from each other, and the idea of universality begins to form. During the third period, the idea of universality is acquired and physical determinism becomes doubled from logical necessity, and *this ends the evolution of the moral obligation of the first stage*.

The first period lasts to the ages of about seven or eight years. During that period there are no natural laws. Physical determinism and moral necessity are completely confused. To put this more precisely, every law which is noticed at work in things is a social law. Things are regarded as acting in conformity with rules which are imposed on them from without. The influence of animism can be traced in this and also of a certain childish artificiality, that is to say a mental tendency to regard everything as having been created by man. Nature is a society of living

[1] Piaget, published by Alcau, Paris, 1927.
In English, Physical Casualty in a Child.

beings of which man is the chief, as well as the creator. Things are under obligation to us—the movement of the sun, of the clouds, and the flowing of the stream. Before the age of seven no example of movement ruled by physical laws is to be found, but there are two motive forces which ensure the movement, an obedient will in that which moves and an external motive force which is, in the first place, man himself, and then certain bodies which act as principals, the sun, for instance, chasing the clouds.

In brief, if there are natural laws, it is simply because things are obedient. For a child natural movements are free movements. A child, previous to that age, constantly attempts to eliminate any element of chance in nature. Even the way in which it asks questions shows that for it everything has a reason for its existence and everything which seems to contradict this conception provokes its curiosity and obliges it to try and find the reason why there are certain quantities or things or events.

No generalization is possible at that period, because everything depends all the time on wills which are included in the things themselves. The water in the rivers usually flows downwards, but it could equally well flow upwards. For the same child one boat may float because it is light and another because it is heavy. The miraculous usually enters into its conception of the world and does so in very familiar fashion (Santa Claus, for example) because everything is reduced to the obedience of things.

In the second stage, starting with the age of seven or eight years, physical determinism makes its appearance. The movement of water and of the clouds is fairly rapidly traced back to mechanical causes: water cannot behave otherwise than flow downhill, a cloud is forced forwards when there is a wind. It is round about the age of eight that the mechanism of a bicycle is thoroughly understood.

A fresh fact is the appearance of the idea of chance which comes to account for strange events, which seem to serve no purpose or are unexpected.

This reducing to physical determinism does not take place equally in every domain, and up to ten or twelve years a number of natural laws are conceived as having a moral nature.

The movement of the sun and the moon is interpreted for the longest time as being in obedience to purely moral laws. It is also frequently the case that the idea of determinism only conquers the details, while the whole preserves a moral aspect. A child will know that rain owes its formation to physical processes, but it will continue to acknowledge that it rains for the sake of the gardens.

This generalization of laws grows in proportion as the idea of a purely moral necessity decreases. Once the movement of rivers has been interpreted physically a child knows that water will always flow downwards. From then onwards it will try to avoid inconsistencies and understands that a law is either a general one or does not exist.

The third period begins round the age of ten to eleven years. The idea of physical determinism is completing its conquests, which come to an end about the age of twelve years, and generalizations reach their full development. But, in proportion as a child renounces the idea of a moral necessity in order to justify laws, it comes to do no more than ascertain that there is a certain generality of facts, which is however without any real foundation; so much, indeed, is this the case, that at that moment it finds itself really impoverished. Yet the evolution continues. The moral necessity of the early years does not disappear without leaving any traces. It becomes gradually transformed into a logical necessity.

Round about the age of ten or eleven the first attempts at deduction and at a logical justification of the laws is to be found, an attitude which becomes developed as time goes on; and thus, by a process of intellectual evolution, the mind is brought back to the obligatory character of the law. At the beginning of its life a child submitted naturally to this obligatory character, and when about twelve years old it has come to understand it. The difference is considerable.

After thinking about this a little, however, a problem arises: how is it that the child had the idea of the obligatory character of the laws, before it knew what they were? How did the child come to this idea of universal obedience, thanks to which it finds itself in the best possible conditions for its mental evolution? At this point we return to the conditions of the obligation of conscience and Bovet traces them directly to the attitude of children in regard to their parents, to that mixture of fear and of love in regard to them, with which they are imbued.

We are thus brought back to the importance of the first years, and if we draw attention, at this stage of our study, to the necessity of looking back, if we would explain the formation of the child, to this special relationship with its parents, it is because, along with the independent researches of Piaget and Bovet, we have ended by establishing a link between a real sense of guilt on the one hand and education in an environment as close as possible to that of the family, on the other.

What is as difficult to explain as a child's belief in universal moral

G

necessity is its disposition towards a sense of guilt, a disposition which seems to be closely bound up with certain forms of education as well as with certain innate tendencies.

We have shown how the logical necessities which are capable of influencing a child remain after all more or less bound up with the stage of moral necessity of the early years. This evolution is never completely finished, but in certain adults it takes place very unsatisfactorily. There are cogent reasons for believing that this failure is closely related with the first years of life, which are the point of departure for all later formations.

III

The evolution of the moral sense in a child deserves our consideration. Here again we shall make use of Piaget's researches, which are explained in detail, giving the methods employed and the results in his work, *Le Jugement moral chez l'enfant.*[1] This evolution of the moral sense can be considered from various points of view, especially from the point of view of the rules of the game. For the sake of clearness we will, however, confine ourselves to the results revealed by more direct investigations.

A very young child up to the age of five or six years practices *moral realism*; that is to say the duties and values which come its way it considers as having an existence of their own and that they impose themselves as binding under all circumstances. This realism has three characteristics:

(a) The duty is essentially imposed from without: every act is good which implies obedience to the rule or even obedience to adults; every act is bad which does not conform to the rules; it is obedience which provides the goodness.

(b) It is the letter and not the spirit of the law which must be observed.

(c) Acts are valued not according to their intention, but according to rules previously laid down.

When it is about twelve years old a child has reached a more or less complete state of moral autonomy. Let us run through with it some of the stages through which it has passed and which will be brought into relief by a particular test.

[1] Moral judgement in children,(Paris, Alcau, 1932).

I. PURELY EXPIATORY PUNISHMENT OR PUNISHMENT BY MUTUAL ACTION (RETALIATION).

A story told by Piaget will shed more light on this question and will help to solve it better than any explanation.

A little boy was playing in his room. His mother asked him to go and fetch some bread for the dinner, because there was none left in the house. Instead of going at once, he answered that it was a bother, but that he would be going in a moment. An hour later he still had not gone and when his father arrived for his dinner there was no bread. The father wondered how he should best punish his little boy. He thought of three punishments. He could stop him going to the circus on the following day, or he could stop him having any bread during dinner, as a piece had since been found in the cupboard; finally, he could say to him, I am not going to punish you, but next time that you ask me to do something for you I shall not do it. Two days later the little fellow wanted a toy which was at the top of the cupboard. He asked his father for this and the latter answered: "You didn't want to help mummy, nor do I want to do anything for you. However, when you are good . . ." Which is the most suitable of the three punishments?

The punishment of being given no bread is clearly an expiatory punishment, whereas the latter is clearly an act of retaliation. A number of stories of this kind could be told and a list made of the children's responses.

Here are the results for questions of this type; the percentage of children who chose *retaliation* has been noted down for each age.

From 6 to 7 years   ..   28%
From 8 to 10 years   ..   49%
From 11 to 12 years   ..   82%

The evolution is very characteristic.

II. INHERENT JUSTICE.

If a child practices this moral realism, can we not bring to light its belief that this sanction is well-founded and universal. Here is one of the stories we are given:

There were once two children who were stealing some apples from a tree. A game-keeper suddenly arrived, and the two children ran away. One was caught. The other made its way home by an out-of-the-way path, crossed the river by a decayed bridge and fell into the water. What do you think about this? If it had not stolen the apples and yet had crossed the river by this decayed bridge, would it then have fallen into the water?

This was the distribution of replies in favour of inherent justice, (If the child had not been stealing it would not have fallen into the water):—

6 years old	86%
From 7 to 8 years old	73%
From 9 to 10 years old	54%
From 11 to 12 years old	34%

We can thus see that in this domain age brings very marked modifications, but the percentage of 34 at twelve years old is still very high. The processes and complexes which are involved in these questions have of course infinitely finer shades and are far more complicated than this extremely schematic history would lead us to suppose. We are here in the main confronted by an attitude which is fundamental in an adult. It is obvious that normally an adult does not expect to be punished by things. But we know at the same time that his sense of guilt makes him conscious, not only of the idea of punishment, but also of the disagreeable little things which happen to him after committing some fault and which it is easy for him to regard as being punishments. The religious attitude is a sublimation of these childish stages, which persist in the subconscious.

III. RETRIBUTIVE JUSTICE AND DISTRIBUTIVE JUSTICE.

These things play an important role in the life of a child, for it is exposed to constant conflicts with adults. May we at this point restrict ourselves to giving a typical situation.

A mother was once walking with her children on the banks of the Rhone, on an afternoon in the holidays. When it was four o'clock, the mother gave each one a little roll. Each one started to eat, except for the smallest, who was careless and let his roll fall into the water. What will the mother do? Should she give him another? What is the opinion of grown-up people?

The answers can be of three types: not to give any more rolls (penalty); to give more so that each may have had one (equality); to give one more because the child is small (equity).

Here we have the distribution of the replies:

		Penalty	Equality	Equity
From 6 to 9 years old	..	48%	35%	17%
From 10 to 12 years old	..	3%	55%	42%
From 13 to 14 years old	..	0%	5%	95%

IV. EQUALITY AND AUTHORITY.

There once was a camp of scouts. Each one had to take his turn at work in order to deal with the various jobs of the camp and to get everything into order. One of them had to do the shopping, another the washing, while another had to collect wood or do the sweeping. It happened that one day there was no more bread left. The boy who was in charge of the shopping had already gone out. The scoutmaster then asked a scout who had already been engaged on some other work to go out and fetch the bread. What did he do?

The replies vary between accepting the job and refusing to do it, as the thing asked for was unjust (equality).

Here is the distribution:

Age		Obedience	Equality
6 years old	..	95%	5%
7 years old	..	55%	45%
8 years old	..	33.3%	66.6%
10 years old	..	10%	90%
12 years old	..	0%	100%

V. IDEAS OF JUSTICE.

Children have been asked to give on their own an example of what is unjust. The replies fall into four classes:

(a) Forms of conduct contrary to the instructions given by adults.
(b) Contrary to the rules of the game.
(c) Contrary to equality.
(d) Forms of injustice relating to the society of adults.

Here is the distribution:

	Forbidden	Game	Inequality	Social Injustice
From 6 to 8 years old	64%	9%	27%	
From 9 to 12 years old	7%	9%	73%	11%

Such are the essential elements which we have borrowed from Piaget concerning the evolution of a child from the ages of six to twelve years. We have seen how this moral evolution, when it has reached a certain state of autonomy, contributes to the evolution of the personality as a whole. Very striking, for instance, is the connection which exists between the intentions and maybe the animism of the child, and the picture which it forms for itself of inherent justice.

It is not necessary, however, to analyse these studies for very long, to become aware that the moral personality which is thus revealed is a "defence" personality without any truly moral character. What we have seen is that *certain conditions for the appearance of a moral life are realized*, but not a moral life itself. Thus the story of the scout who refused to go and fetch the bread because this was not his job could only with difficulty be compared with a true moral attitude. It is obvious that we could only speak of a moral life if, under such conditions, the scout went to fetch the bread, even if this was an injustice, and we could not then speak of true autonomy. The word autonomy can always be used when the elaboration of the moral judgment comes from the actual person, and is not automatically accepted from without.

Furthermore, researches which have been made by Mlle J. De Clerck in regard to pupils in college, aged from ten to eighteen years, with a view to establishing certain norms which could be used as tests, have shown that the general emotional organization of a child of ten years does not differ seriously from that of a young man of eighteen or twenty years. We cannot describe here the method followed, but it touches on certain fundamental points. We can, however, see that at the age of ten and even of twelve years a boy is not yet capable of a real and a deep friendship (taken as a whole). This capacity will only come to him with puberty.

We also see that this same child of ten years shows, on the average, a preference for its mother, though this is not stressed; it will indeed not be stressed for a few years yet. Its sentiments in regard to its father are, on the average, also not stressed. It is only round about the age of fourteen years that it starts to bring an impartial judgment to bear.

From that age onwards, for example, it can be seen showing its preference for its mother, while attributing to its father a sense of greater justice. From then on it becomes capable of judging between two values.

As for its powers of resentment or its sense of justice, these already show themselves, from the age of ten years, under the same fundamental forms as in an adult. It would not seem that after that much progress is achieved. An important element which should always be remembered is that when ten years old, it is only able to make a sympathetic exception in the case of its parents, whereas a little later it will be able to do so for some person whom it loves; its aggressive instincts cease to function as regards this person, by reason of friendship or love.

★　　★　　★

We have seen then that it is not only at puberty, as is generally believed, that autonomous judgment appears in a child. This autonomy is to be found much earlier and there is no doubt that we should bear this in mind.

A child judges its parents, and in very definite fashion, from the age of eight or ten years; it may indeed make mistakes but nevertheless it passes judgment. In every case it is important that it should not have too much that is well-founded with which to reproach them. It judges its superiors. It also judges the persons whose story it is told. We know of more than one adult in whom a religious crisis was started owing to facts described in the Bible and especially certain little facts in the Gospels, such as the story of Jesus remaining with the doctors of the law, while his mother was seeking for him anxiously. There are numbers of children, in fact, who cannot help seeing that such an act, when judged from their own viewpoint, is not right; as regards this detail, and indeed many others which we have not the space to quote here, it would be wise to take care, when presenting these facts to childish minds, to explain to them how, in the long run, they will be found to rest on sound foundations. This is not always easy, and we become aware of this after reading the interpretations which François Mauriac gives of some of these events.

Religious instruction, as it evolves, should anyway to a large extent follow the development of the children; it should follow it, make use of it, and give it both a meaning and a unity. This is what we propose to study in the next chapter.

CHAPTER SEVEN

The School and the First Meeting with God

I

When speaking of meeting with God, we shall confine ourselves to following what takes place in the soul of a child, at the school and the catechism age, when, if its educational formation is sufficient, Christ and God become formative elements in its thought, collaborating in the shaping of its personality.

This account of the formative rôle played by God and by the person of Christ in the moral flowering of a child, which would seem to us to be an indispensable complement of all education, has not been the object of special scientific research.

The reader must be warned of this and must realize that we here give no more than an essay, based on certain experiments and on sufficient fundamental principles, but which has not received, if we may so put it, any official consecration. This essay is a kind of summary of our study of the moral sense in individuals, a study which it is unfortunately difficult to present in a strictly scientific fashion. May we add that the Freudian interpretation of Christ, which we are quite unable to accept as satisfactory, has urged us to go rather more deeply into this question, for it has a way of trying to find its solution in that direction.

Those who picture the "moral sense" or the "moral consciousness" as a simple function, with but one voice, are probably making a mistake.

In the consciousness of a child of seven years there exists a certain picture of its personality, a picture given by the description which it receives from its environment. This environment may describe it as being courageous, timid, a thief, good or bad, compassionate or selfish, intelligent or dull-witted, etc., etc.; the child gets a glimpse of itself through the medium of these words. One thing then comes first: the idea that the world forms of it. But this idea does not fill its consciousness, for this also has in it at the same time the idea that the child has of itself. These two ideas do not overlap, for, on the one hand, the child may be reproached for faults which it does not believe it has or which it does not have, or on the other hand, it may also be credited with qualities which it does not possess to such a degree. There is thus added to what already exists in its child's unconsciousness the desire to be judged by the world in a satisfactory way, and for this reason it wishes to see the world behave in a certain way. A child wishes at the same time to be judged in a satisfactory way, and yet at the same time to give the world the opportunity to appreciate it at its true value; this means that it is conscious of the need for behaving in a certain way, according to the idea which it has formed of itself.

Now, after that, in so far as it has formed the habit of trying to do its best, and to act with sincerity, or else has formed the habit of feigning a certain line of conduct, it will wish to see the world behaving in a more discerning way, so that it may be appreciated at its true value, or it may on the other hand be afraid lest someone should possess this power of discernment. The child will in any case be led on to the possibility of seeing the world it knows replaced by a more discerning world, and it will in consequence be led on to desire or to fear a being more perfect than can be found in this world (its parents and its environment), where it meets with such poor judgment. Such a desire would, no doubt, never come to the surface of its mind, even in a rudimentary way, if it did not already know that the little Jesus, that mysterious being who up to then has explained everything, is all-powerful. It goes without saying that in most cases a child hopes for and at the same time dreads the existence of an observer superior to its surroundings, and the theme of the little Jesus, which will gradually become transformed into a more precise idea, following a child's evolution till it reaches the idea of pure spirit, will clearly take the place of that of its parents, its environment and the world. Besides, when a child hears God described as infinitely just, knowing everything, seeing everything, and able to do everything, it will not be particularly astonished and will have no difficulty in accepting this: without being conscious of the fact, it needed such a being.

When, a few years later, an adolescent or a man may even deny the existence of God, it will be most often by making appeal to its childish desires which have at that time been disappointed: "—No, I do not believe in God; if there was a God, he would not let me be treated as he has done; there would not be so much injustice, there would be more pity in the world. . . . ."—Such blasphemies are in fact no more than the realization that God, as such children knew Him, has not assumed the rôle which it had been hoped He would play, has not responded to their reasons for believing. This also proves that the childish picture, which they had formed of God either failed to evolve or else was not understood by their educators.

The more primitive societies can only put before children extremely human gods, of very diverse natures, responding at the same time to what they dread and what they desire. Fear is clearly in the ascendant and a child can only finish up with an elementary mythology, with the practical means of appeasing the anger of these gods and even attracting their good graces. The later evolution of such a child ceases too soon, and moves in one direction only: learning magical practices which may prove useful.

In societies which are still primitive but have evolved rather further, monotheism may be found: there is a desire for a single deity which unites in itself alone and in a pre-eminent degree the particular dispositions of a number of divinities. We have here an intellectual creation, difficult for a childish intelligence to grasp, and we must limit ourselves to describing certain qualities which would be particularly interesting to a child: omniscience, omnipresence, justice, infinite goodness and above all, omnipotence.

Now, we should take special note of this, because it is a very important fact: the God who is pure spirit, the origin of all things, omniscient and omnipresent, of incorruptible justice, *surpasses the real needs of a child.*

A child feels itself crushed before such a being, powerless, and compelled to adopt a form of behaviour which would not impose itself in this way, if this God whose existence is revealed to it at some special moment were not felt to be above it to an extraordinary extent.

A child will, in consequence, easily content itself with simpler gods. On the one hand it will be able, like the children of primitive peoples, to satisfy itself with secondary divinities, which are easy or more easy to approach, and there is unfortunately in existence a way of presenting Catholicism to children which is not far removed from a form of fairly rudimentary polytheism. We need not dwell on this subject; we only wish to point out the danger, which is all too real a one, of teaching a Catholicism of inferior quality, which will certainly be attractive to children and will produce immediate results, but will founder during the synthetic period of puberty with little hope of returning. It will not in fact be Catholicism which has become extinguished in that intelligence, but its teachers, with the best intentions, will have stifled all possibility in that soul of true Catholicism, by impoverishing, with puerile and facile secondary cults, the very idea of God.

On the other hand, a child may without becoming involved in this dispersive action, meet with a single God who is much closer at hand! This is the totalitarian idol, whether race, country or perhaps even a little above this, the whole of humanity. The school can reveal to a child that there is a social organization superior to the environment in which it lives, better informed, more powerful, more just. It will not need to go so far as God the Spirit in order to find satisfaction. It will find, within its reach so to speak, a very satisfying answer. And as the idea of God, no matter under what form, responds in a certain sense to a necessity, to a thoroughly real need, and as this God, the "social organization," is accessible to its requests and gives it satisfaction in simple fashion, a child is likely to accept it completely and will even make use of it as an ally against family discipline. The informations lodged by children in totalitarian states against their parents are expressions of that evolution, of that need to have recourse to some external power so as to obtain help in an illusory peril. We do not have to give this matter much thought in order to see that by satisfying, between the ages of nine and ten years, by some national, racial or humanitarian myth, the impulse which, by the force of circumstances, a child has taken towards God, the proud response which it could give to the pure doctrine of monotheism, can be ruined, and maybe for ever; the child's first opportunity for meeting with God has been set aside, all for the sake of a myth. This new God will be able to teach them about himself in those schools in which the children will be formed, he will have the same title to do so as philosophy, the sciences and history, but he will not be revealed to the child as a liberation towards the infinite. In such schools, God becomes a scholarly acquirement. The God whom the child desired has been given to him under the form of a certain material organization of life, an organization of which God forms part. It is not difficult to understand that the apparent respect for a divinity which has been annexed by some national or racial myth really has no value whatsoever. Such a structure might carry a Catholic label, but it has really left no place for God.

As we have seen, we find in the moral consciousness of a child, which is in a state of constant evolution, alongside the desire or the fear of seeing the world acting in a certain way, a picture of its own behaviour in regard to the group to which it belongs and in regard to what it has substituted for the group.

But the picture which the individual, in this case the child, has of its own behaviour is by no means a simple thing. It is specially aware of how it would behave if it could behave as it would like; of the behaviour it must adopt if it wishes to be accepted with complete approval by its environment; of that which it would like to see authorized by its environment and of that which it thinks it should adopt when faced with that being which it has been extremely fortunate to meet with outside its environment; for at the same time as there is revealed to it a judge who is inexorable in the eyes of those around, the child comes under the eyes of the same inexorable judge. The moral conscience is not formed till a child can act and think in connection with all these elements, notably *in connection with its view of God, which should not be different from that of its own conscience.*

Naturally, the moral conscience gives its characteristic structure or organization at the same time, through the child's experience, by the examples set before it, by the habits and inhibitions created in it.

We have, up to now, only met the God of every monotheistic religion, (and we have seen how difficult it is to reach him, and how easy to lose the way, even in the very heart of Catholicism), but we have not yet come in contact with Christianity. Christ introduces into the conscience, by being an example and a pattern, a way of universal behaviour both in regard to the world and in regard to the Divinity. And as, in the pattern of a child's moral consciousness, the Divinity tends to take the place of the material world, so does the personality of Christ tend, in the same moral consciousness, to replace all the pictures of self of which we have been speaking, by a form of behaviour based on an ideal pattern. But as nobody reaches the point of seeing only God in the world, even so nobody succeeds in completely letting Christ take the place of his own consciousness; this is nevertheless the basis of the problem, and this structure of the conscience should be firmly established, (which does not mean that it need be conscious), at the end of the school and the catechism periods. On this basis all the later moral evolution of the individual will be built. Should it be missing it is clear enough that some other thing will have taken its place.

That other thing which, in the formation of a conscience, takes the place of Christ, will not always be completely contrary to the pattern set before us by the Gospels, and may at times come very close to it, but under another name. There is nothing to prevent us thinking of a conscience with Christian leanings, but which does not know that it is Christian, being more perfect than one which is said to be Christian, but which is really the expression of a thoroughly mediocre Christ. In the same way, when speaking from the psychological point of view, an atheist, at one period of his life, may have experienced states of soul sufficient to lead him to God, and while his response may seem to be atheistic, as long as such states of soul remain in force, nevertheless we can still find ourselves in face of points of view which can be described as religious. Anyway, however this may be, true Christianity does not begin till one way of life is placed before a child and virtually accepted, to the exclusion of every other solution.

There are two types which stand in special opposition to each other, the type which we may call Caesarian and the Christian type.

One of the most famous murderers of recent years, in his personal papers, picturing an interview with himself, asks this question:

"If you were not yourself, who would you wish to be?"

And he answers himself: "God, who is all wisdom, all greatness, all knowledge, all power." Nothing can give us a better idea than this answer of the meaning and the symbolism of the revolt of the Angels. One of the most natural errors is that of picturing an effort to be identified with God, to be on the same level with Him, as a normal mode of behaviour. If monotheism may be in one sense a response of almost universal character to certain psychological dispositions, which we found at an early age in children, the assimilation of the subject itself to God can be almost fatal, if everything works out in a spontaneous way. When we know the special power of the instinct of the ego, of the instinct for domination, of that "will to power" which swells the hearts of men, we can easily imagine where such an assimilation may end.

Furthermore, as the history of religions has proved, monotheism as such has not necessarily a particular moral value; it is even compatible with every sort of deviation. The fact that an individual ends by identifying himself more or less completely with the God of Hosts, who having been socially transformed, becomes a simple being at the service of some community, gives him a certain moral liberation, the liberation of the ego in almost every direction. Pantheism in particular lends itself to such an evolution, and in this matter the cult of nature is even more fertile, whilst the deification of the race, the nation or of humanity definitely postulate it. The only God which a scholar of what we may call a Caesarian régime will really know will be that quasi-material being (even if he has a nominal knowledge of God the Spirit), since his material God suffices for his general aspirations, and his adoration of this God will be all the more easy and complete in that he will in a certain sense form part of this God. And it is at the moment when Christ can enter into a soul and move it in a Christian direction that a child will be given the emblem of a spear or some such thing, in essential opposition to the doctrine of Christ. It has been said that in principle this child sacrifices itself for the community which has thus been deified, but this is psychologically meaningless: for a child the idea of its total disappearance is unthinkable, and when at that age it makes the virtual sacrifice of its life, it has in no sense realized, even from a distance, the fulness of this sacrifice. On the other hand, to brandish a spear in order to make the earth tremble is something very clear and plain, and of a kind to fascinate the souls of all the children in the world.

Few educators, even among Catholics, take into account the elementary psychological fact that a monotheistic God of the Caesarian type or the communist myth, or the myth of Roman universality, or that of Germanism, give to their faithful the same satisfaction of the power instinct. The discipline imposed by these doctrines on certain sides draws near to Christian and Catholic morality, and yet they are essentially inferior forms of morality, when compared with Christianity. Being unaware of this, there are many educators who give far too much place to this will to power, to force and to domination, in the upbringing of children, tendencies which are so interesting to children but so contradictory to the personality of Christ.

The spear is significant of all monotheism of the Caesarian type, for hatred is the faithful companion of the instinct for domination; and we have seen how resentment is one of the reasons which incite a child not to be content with its surroundings as they are. Resentment and hatred (which is really no more than the organization of resentment, abandoning oneself to it) will remain one of the great driving forces of that diverted form of the cult of the ego which makes up "Caesarian" theism.

Now, a child is particularly prone to resentment, on account of the inferior position in holds in regard to the rest of society, and also because it has not yet learnt (and it will always try not to have to learn) how to free itself, at least partially, from its emotional states; it has not learnt how to drown those sentiments which should be kept in the background.

Fortunately, there exists in a child, in opposition to its desire for domination and its constant tendency towards resentment, an unbounded love of all living things, an improbable aptitude for endowing animals and objects with a love like its own and to hold communion with all things in sympathy and love. This unconscious, instinctive love of things can provide a serious emotional basis for the love of its neighbour. And it is very probable, if not almost certain, that love for its neighbour and, at the same time, love for God, will be grafted onto this universal sympathy of a child, bringing order to it and setting it within bounds. In our day education, being based on the domination of nature and of creatures, tends to extinguish at an early age this communion which a child holds with things, and to do so more and more. Nowadays, there are already at the age of ten many children who could no longer give their whole souls to Christ, as far as their affections are concerned; they have already lost the habit of universal love which came naturally to them in their early years.

Christ, by bringing it love, gives order in the soul of a child to all this diffuse sympathy. Christ sets before us the love of our neighbour in God, and wishes to lead the movement of love beyond resentment and the desire to dominate. He even proposes the love of enemies and has himself given an example of this.

If it is true that resentment can lead to a certain just balance, it is by love that Christ wishes to form the child's sense of justice. This universal love, this justice based on the gift of self and not on the dispossession of another, is not to be learnt by young children in abstract terms, but they live these things when they hear the Gospel stories. Is there any child that is not astonished at seeing Christ not using force, and even refusing to have a sword used in his defence? At the first onset no child accepts this attitude which is perfect above all others, indeed it perhaps never accepts it completely, and Christianity will never be more to it than a model set before it for its behaviour, a model of which it will never achieve the perfection. The history of Christ brings to a child in the middle of its formation the idea that its destiny must be accepted, the idea of complete love, of never hurting other people, of submission to higher laws than those which the ego discovers or accepts. And because Christ is Himself all strength and all power, though this strength and power are only shown in the infinite gift of self, a child, by becoming absorbed in Christ, can satisfy its aspirations towards the infinite, but to an infinite which will only show itself by the submission and surrender of its own self, and which will flower in the highest forms of love.

There is thus a Christian conception of the world, which answers to the fundamental disposition of the human being. These fundamental dispositions can furthermore become organized without coming into contact with Christ, as all the world knows, and there are numerous non-Christian societies in which love of the neighbour is not lacking. Christ presents this love in a supreme form.

But, just as we can find a certain neighbourly love organized outside Christianity, it is possible to find thoroughly bad examples of this love right within Christianity, and it is not really saying anything new to point out that, in the very heart of Christianity, the attempts that we make to try and bring Christ to life in the souls of children are at times of very mediocre quality. If theoretical teaching is the same everywhere, practical teaching is often very far from Christ; in everything apart from definitely religious lessons, teachers think and speak all too often as simple believers of the Caesarian type.

Without dwelling on the resentment which certain forms of education try and awaken in a child, against the Jews and the "Enemies" of religion, we cannot fail to observe how few teachers teach and practice, we need not say love but simply respect for an adversary, how few of them point out that symbolic charity in the form of an alms which costs the donor nothing has no Christian value, how few imagine that the essence of Christianity is to be found beyond the rite that is laid down and that Christ must be taught, not as He has become within us in the course of our evolution, with all our dryness and our denials, but as He really was, as representing the most beautiful type of humanity, as the most perfect realization of human faculties in this world. Christ does not set before us a Caesar—God, victorious over this world, but a man accepting the laws of his condition as man with human perfection.

Thus, as we have seen, God and Christ can at a certain moment make themselves known to the moral consciousness, to the personality of the child. It is between the ages of six and twelve years that receptivity is most alive to the fundamental patterns of ideal conduct. We often think of the children of other religions who do not know Christ. We must also think how Christ knows the Catholic children in their own schools. Our pious reviews tell us of the number of pilgrimages, of conversion statistics and other encouraging things; there are, however, reasons for asking ourselves whether Catholics and even Christians are nowadays worthy of their mission, if they have not stifled the primitive aspiration for their personal profit. In Holland, where it is possible to make the comparison, crime amongst Catholics reaches the figure of 406.5 for 100,000 inhabitants; that of Protestants is 308.6, of Jews 212.7, and of unbelievers 84.2. We must certainly avoid exaggerating the significance of these figures, but the digression is very large; it proves conclusively that the fact of being labelled Catholic or Christian does not in itself signify very much, and that the moral perfection of the doctrine may be most imperfectly realized in the characters of the believers.

All we have tried to do has been to show that the personality of a child turns fairly naturally towards God and towards Christ, who exist for it under the form of needs and of aspirations, but that perfection in teaching and in methods and above all perfection in the teachers will play a considerable rôle; that a child's first meeting with God should not be limited to consolidating its elementary dispositions, but should end by forming a definite order in the mind, which should be able to improve indefinitely these passing stages.

From this point of view, the reproach which is sometimes made against Christianity that its contacts with life are from too great a distance is perhaps not without a certain foundation. The defence organization against the excesses of sexuality partly explains this attitude. On the other hand, it is around the ages of nine, ten or twelve years that real sexual difficulties can begin in a child, though this may happen earlier or sometimes later. Now, when a child feels that it is guilty, those in charge of it should take care to prevent it believing that it is no longer worthy of human companionship, but that, on the contrary, it should maintain its affectionate contact with every form of life. And it is important that, whatever it may entail, a child should then know that it will never be set aside, but that it will always remain loved by Christ with an unshakable love.

We are not sure if we have made it sufficiently understood that in the experience of life, which a child undergoes round about the time at school, in the course of which it develops according to a general pattern, God and Christ will come before it, not as abstract entities, but as models. It tries to place itself in the place of these models; it tries to identify itself with them; but also to bring them back to its own level. The face of Christ appears to a child to be essentially human and near to it, and this is no doubt a good thing, but one which also enables it to estimate the conduct of other human beings which its own observation or the force of circumstances have revealed to it. A child thus "tries on," so to speak, all the models which are set before it, just as it attempts a large number of different types of writing.

Theoretical Christian teaching, which is, however, contradicted in practice by the behaviour of those who give it, only penetrates the soul of a child as something that is written down, but not as an element forming part of its personality.

It is certainly agreed on all sides that nobody can reproduce in himself a really worthy Christ, and that from a certain point of view the work of a teacher would seem to be the most formidable of any. But we all know how certain teachers would, like the Jews of old, wish to have an autocratic Christ; we all know the reverses which the love of our neighbour and the principle of human fraternity have to undergo, due to passing circumstances. Nevertheless Christ lived in a time of social upheaval and remained serenely fraternal.

Finally, we know all too well the contempt which many teachers have for that flowering of sympathy in a child towards all things: beasts and plants, the clouds, the sky and the sun. These great reserves of affection should be allowed to develop, for they will later on be transferred quite naturally. It is necessary to insist on the fact that the formation of the moral sense in a child is independent of certain magical and utilitarian practices, or of some which are merely superstitious. Unfortunately, for a very large number of believers, religion is nothing more than a means of making sure of receiving favours in this world and in the other, by means of fulfilling certain obligations, of observing certain restrictions and performing certain external acts. For a child, it is all too often the means of obtaining extra marks or perhaps the occasion for losing them: the number of Masses and of Holy Communions here come in as a form of currency. Certainly, all this may not be blameworthy, but has only a distant connection with the most complete, the most disinterested and the most freely bestowed gift that any man has ever made of himself.

On the other hand, the Christianising of the personality has to be in accordance with a child's temperament, with its intelligence, its emotional reactions, the environment in which it lives, the amount of injustice to which it submits or thinks it has to submit, the amount of resentment which it has to overcome, the number of opportunities that it has of turning towards other creeds than that of Christianity; and owing to the fact that each child represents a different organism and a different history, doctrine cannot exist in the same form in every man, but can only influence them more or less, according to a general pattern.

A school will have been of real service to a child if it has put it in a condition to be able to communicate with all men and with the whole of creation, but has also provided it with a moral framework which is truly universal and a way of behaving which is the best that humanity can attain. As it grows older, it will try and escape from this moral order, but the school must do nothing to assist or to prepare for such a breaking away.

It has been said, and Jean-Jacques formulated this idea quite clearly, that the absolutely perfect Christian would be an essentially amorphous being, in that he would submit to the worst without rebellion, would be prepared to look on the worst of misfortunes as a blessing, and the most elementary good things of this world would fail to interest him. We do not know how far such an objection can be said to be relevant, but are inclined to believe that there are Christians who would be inclined to consider that it contains a certain amount of truth.

For our part, viewing the matter from the biological and psychological point of view, we do not see how we could meet this objection which has meaning only if one has in view a perfect man who is able to follow completely a code of life which is imposed on him from without, with his own personality counting for nothing. On the plane of reality, however, such a man does not exist. The instinct for power, human and sexual passions, the need for affectionate relations with other people, give a man an aggressive and dynamic quality; he can no more prevent himself facing the problems which come before him than he can avoid, from the moral point of view, creating an order which will accord with all his experience. Life is just that. Now, Christianity does not replace the foundation of the personality, but is added to it, yet it can only be received by the individual after undergoing, as it enters into him, a certain deformation, a certain adaptation to the elements which are there already; it is never the whole of the individual.

Furthermore, at no moment of life is it really understood in all its greatness, on account of man's infirmity and his constant lack of experience. In short, even in the best-disposed man, Christianity is never realized except in a most partial and intermittent way, and then as a corrective of his tendencies towards domination and egotism.

It is this corrective, helping the human attitude to improve when faced with life, which gives us some idea of the contribution of Christianity to civilized life. Unfortunately, after the two thousand years during which this "corrective" has been evolving, it would not seem that the danger of having to deal with men who are too perfect has drawn any nearer. It is more or less as if we were to say that there exists enough Christianity in the world for a certain maintenance of civilization. It may be that the words "You are the salt of the earth" should be understood in a very humble sense. This combination of a general betterment can only be obtained by means of individual betterments; but whereas *science can be taught all ready-made, as left to us by the previous generation, the moral sense is above all an individual formation, which each man must undertake from the beginning. The standpoint of previous generations will only serve as a pattern, without really affecting its own evolution.* Thus the school and the catechism, do not create a new personality, they merely play a part in its formation.

Christianity gives men the chance to escape from their latent animal qualities; they will, however, have already made a spontaneous effort to break loose from these fundamental animal characteristics, and Christianity does not become triumphant until it begins to illuminate, in majestic fashion, far beyond any human capacity, this effort at liberation of which we have already given an rough sketch. We are also too ready to forget that even this human weakness exerts an influence on doctrine and it is not impossible to imagine a form of Christianity which has been reduced to human dimensions. It would not be difficult to prove that this is all too often the case, and that there are many schools, even Catholic ones, which have formed mentalities that are only Christian in name, mentalities, that is to say, which regard Christianity as no more than a collection of mediocre moral qualities, to be found amongst all men, mentalities in which every flame has already been extinguished, even at the threshold of puberty. Christianity does not begin till we meet the good Samaritan. A child is able to understand this parable, by reason of which, if the lesson is well taught, it will make a secret examination of its habits. A child cannot, however, understand how Christ could let Himself be put to death, He who is all-powerful, without resisting for one moment; it cannot understand how he had to sheathe the sword which could have effected his escape. This extraordinary attitude leaves a permanent mark on its mind, something inimitable and mysterious, fascinating and at the same time inadmissible, something which really disturbs its conscience. It feels that it will never accept such greatness, and yet is unwilling to admit that it is definitely incapable of doing so. Fortunate is the child which can take away from school, along with its dream of love, this secret resistance to this unheard-of sacrifice, but at the same time the idea that that is where perfection is to be found.

CHAPTER EIGHT

Adolescence
The Age of Independence

I

Primary schools can do no more than produce normal children once they have reached the age of from twelve to thirteen years. The programme is drawn up for childish minds and fails to satisfy intelligences which have been emancipated and awakened. Besides, at the present day, children who have to complete their education at a primary school lose part of their last years.

Every attempt is made, before they leave, to confine them within the limits of the manuals used. The teacher who instructed them in figures was himself unaware that tens of thousands of years had to go by before men had learnt to make use of the figure o, and to have the idea of placing a comma between the decimal units. The child will never know that what he learnt at school is the extraordinary gift of all the men who preceded him on the earth and that the multiplication table is not something discovered at random by the schools' inspectors.

The poor boy leaves school full of boredom and disgust, his chief desire being to get rid of all that and really to start living. A certain number will come to maturity in the professional schools and will speak of the watt, the volt and the ampère without realizing that these are derived from the names of real people.

It is sometimes asked whether a trade should be chosen following an examination or a test? A thousand times no! With a view to some given trade, it is necessary to possess a certain minimum aptitude for it; this can be measured by means of a test and the result should certainly be taken into account. But this testing should be no more than a negative element (we might call it a counter-indication) and does not become a positive or unique factor in making the choice: this would mean the complete denial of the human personality, and we know that the free choice of ways of life is usually the climax of a long series of interior events. Only laboratory psychologists are unaware of or neglect this essential element in the choice. And it is because in orphanages or charity schools the children lack this long series of inner events which leads to the choice of a trade, that they are seldom to be found, once they have come out, doing the type of work which they learnt when they were inmates.

In the case of those who finish their instruction in a primary school, adolescence and puberty fix them for all time in certain elementary positions, and they gradually join the rank and file, take their place among them, and start representing their family at funerals. A few among them may become councillors, but only one in ten thousand will become a Claude Bernard.[1] There is to be found, however, an unknown richness of adaptations, of sacrifices, of wisdom and of happiness as well, in the vast group of those we have just been discussing. Life is good among them. They know all the proverbs and all the sayings, they live in close relationship with commonsense, with practical and first-hand certainties; they are ready for every trial, and have a pragmatic philosophy which, with a benevolent assurance of being in agreement with their creator, is always ready to censure their parish priest's sermons, when they are too severe.

In what are called the young countries, in which the State never leaves go of human beings from the cradle to the grave, adolescence is skilfully exploited. This finds its achievement in the willingness to raise clenched fists or extended arms, working together as a group, while crying out some slogan. And, according to one's own temperament or experience, one finds that such young characters are healthy or are alarming.

II

When making the retrospective analysis of an adult personality, an essential, if not perhaps the most important point, is to know whether, at a special moment, such a man made the gift of himself, even if only partially. Puberty sets the limits within which a man will be able to escape from himself, to sacrifice part of himself to other people; puberty will decide whether he will live as a more or less complete parasite, or whether he will collaborate with the community. Puberty, furthermore, only acts on a mentality as it has been formed by its upbringing in childhood, and a man may be ruined even before he reaches adolescence; it also only acts on a constitution which has already been formed, and the organic phenomena which determine its nature differ in intensity and rapidity from one being to another; finally, the chances for a favour-

[1] A celebrated French physiologist who has been described as the most illustrious representative of experimental science in the second half of the nineteenth century.

able evolution are confined to cases of normal physiological evolution; no education can fill the need caused by organic deficiencies, or can prevent the shipwreck of the finest mind, if puberty leads on to dementia. Above all, nothing can prevent hereditary mental disorder from revealing itself clearly at this unstable period or from disturbing those mental accomplishments which seemed to have reached solidity. Just because it is a period of transformation and of life, adolescence is fragile, it is sensitive to the smallest influences. *At the moment when he is of an age to give himself freely, with the illusion that his judgment is absolutely reliable, a young man has the smallest powers of resistance and is most open to suggestion,* and that is why he has always been the spoilt child of social movements, or the favourite prey of the latest idols.

Puberty begins at about twelve, thirteen or fourteen years, and comes slowly to completion. If it is easy to decide when it starts, for this is an abrupt change in that rapidity of growth which has often been going on for a year or two, changing the features, causing various organic changes so as to produce the complete male or female physique, it is far more difficult to say where it ends. The end can be delayed till the age of seventeen, eighteen, twenty or even twenty-one years. It is usually held that the unhealthy surroundings of towns hastens its evolution, but we should beware of such summary estimates. The psychical aspect of puberty is certainly more difficult to estimate than its organic changes, and we may say that it is on the mental side that the boundaries of the effects of puberty are hardest to define. Furthermore, it is not possible, in such a special subject, the moral evolution of which cannot be followed from close quarters, to state precisely, from the psychological standpoint, where adolescence begins or where it ends. The modifications which take place overlap each other; childish attitudes do not cease to exist but become transformed. Puberty makes use of the materials which are already there and reveals itself through them. The changes which it brings, no matter how deep they may go, will follow the line which comes down from childhood. If this childhood had been an unfortunate one, puberty will never be able to put this right; it may indeed make matters worse. The same change will take place later on, with the passage to mature age, and the man will be no more than what the adolescent was potentially.

The crisis in behaviour is generally the most striking thing, and it is often believed that this crisis brings puberty to an end. What is taken to be the crisis in behaviour is usually no more than the prelude. The crisis in behaviour in the exact sense of the word, is the crisis of disobedience and insubordination which arises between the ages of twelve and fourteen years, on an average at thirteen years; it shows itself in the reports of those who are at a boarding-school, while those who are living at home reveal it by acts of indiscipline which can go quite a long way, sometimes even leading to the children's court. In actual fact this state of still very childish excitement, this state of blind resistance aimed at every check which up to then has been accepted, really belongs to a neutral moment between childhood and puberty itself. At that moment, under the influence of certain glands which are giving virility to its muscular system, and the nervous system, which reveals its strength and incites it to constant exercise, a child (for it still has a childish mentality), plays at being a man, it sets up a resistance, it admires itself because it is robust and rapid in movement, it feels that it could easily overcome the physical strength of those it has feared up to then. At the same time a strong sense of physical well-being, an increase of good health, makes it incapable of remaining in one place; it also notices that it finds physical pain far more bearable than it used to, and that it can no longer be restrained as was previously the case. We now have before us the well-known picture of the schoolboy with long arms and bony hands, who laughs at his sisters and laughs at established custom, who tears his clothes, throws things at the pictures, eats ravenously, and roars with laughter at everything in such a thoughtless way that he earns a good deal of adverse judgment.

This disobedience, this lack of restraint in movement, these exhibitions which, to speak the truth, can sometimes be intolerable, will not last. In the normal course of events, everything, after a year or two, will be in order once again and one would imagine that it was all over. This physical insubordination will only continue in a few cases, and these will be the least gifted, casting considerable doubts on the boy's social capacities. The true crisis in behaviour, in most normal young people, is entirely an interior matter, and leads them on to a revision of the moral code to which they have submitted so far. It is only when the solution which a young man reaches as the result of this revision causes a rupture between him and his environment that a different form of behaviour and a different moral attitude will reveal themselves. It will no longer be a matter of disobedience, but of revolt, of a revolt that will be either healthy or harmful according to whether it is caused by accepting a higher ideal or sets the seal on a falling away. This, however, marks the final stage, and we must return to the things which make up the crisis of disobedience.

III

In reality, this period of disobedience which calls for other methods than those which up to then have been used to keep a child within the bounds of order, coincides with a certain insensibility to pain, which is mental rather than physical; there is a functional perfection of the senses, which has not been previously attained and will not come again, with a very real control of the muscular system by the will. It is the age when a boy places himself above physical pain, he learns not to cry if he receives a knock, and this change goes with the disappearance—which has been envisaged for some time—of infantile ways of expressing emotion. At the same time, a little after the disappearance of fear when faced with physical pain, there appears for the first time in a conscious form the capacity for controlling moral fear, a capacity which produces a marked improvement in the domain of inhibitions, the beginning of the submission of the emotional life to the will. This awakes in him the certainty of being able to rely on himself, for he is now master of himself, and can express himself socially *by what can really be called courage*. From then onwards it is possible to speak of will and self-control.

In a certain number of primitive societies, what are known as initiation ceremonies take place round about the ages of sixteen or eighteen years, a little earlier or a little later according to racial customs and characteristics; these are no more than tests of courage, in the course of which a young man must be able to bear, in virile fashion, the physical sufferings imposed on him by the ceremonies, and must control his emotional reflexes. If he does not succeed in this, he is not considered as fit for sharing in the life of men. This is an excellent way of diagnosing any emotional backwardness, of whatever kind it may be. This persistence of childish reactions at an age when they should have become transformed is specially to be found among those in whom, by force of anatomical or physiological conditions, the evolution of puberty has not been completed. It is only in societies which are already fairly civilized, in which the courage of the community can make up for the failings of individuals, that the elimination of the backward and childish no longer takes place.

Self-confidence, both in the intellectual and physical domains, issues naturally from such a state of affairs and it is round about this period that the first personal judgments (which are anyway regarded as personal creations by their author) make their impress on the mind and give a fresh interpretation to the past. This disposition soon forms in the mind a kind of condensed encyclopedia, of those things which should be retained and seen again; everything which had been accepted without discussion up to then is assessed once more, and is laid open to being accepted again or to being rejected. Now, the unique value of such thought lies in self-confidence and in its sincerity. A young man is unaware of his utter poverty, and he would consider himself insulted if he heard it affirmed. Thanks to this poverty, which, however, allows him to think of the positive and the absolute, his personality is exposed to every influence, provided that they are at work without his being aware of it, that they allow him to form his own judgment, and satisfy the fundamental aspirations which are beginning to reveal themselves in him.

The most noticeable consequence of all this is the emancipation of the young man from his family circle. At the same time that he has shed his childish reactions, he has also broken loose from that constant guardianship of his mind which was exercized by his family, and has difficulty in bearing with it. Perhaps he is not thinking differently than he was before, but he is now thinking on his own and he is discovering the world, he is also transferring to society, though without being aware of the fact, those powers which up to then he has only recognized in his nearest relations. However, his need of paternal or maternal approval has not disappeared. He soon experiences the same need in regard to people who represent bodies having a wider scope than the boundaries of his home: local, national and international corporations; religion, and even people representing ideas, such as humanity, justice and beauty. If he is religious, God begins to play another part in his life than that of providing interests, and ends by becoming the centre of his evolution . . . . but generosity, in his relations with God, at first has only an unobtrusive rôle. If it is left to itself for most of the time, it will never reach maturity. The adolescent who feels that he is quite naturally immortal—he still needs time in order to become aware that death is much nearer than he believes—who feels that he is powerful, gifted with new and assured thoughts, likes to think he has been chosen by God, but in reality in a completely pagan way. It is the idea which he has of himself which causes this strange association. Almost all adolescents have dreams of grandeur. Georges Dumas, who collected the confidential statements of numerous schoolboys, written under the promise of secrecy, saw this well: riches, glory, power, the love and admiration of others, form the secret and unacknowledged preoccupation of these young people and the approval which they receive from God or from men whom they love or admire, is first of all understood as setting a seal on their pre-eminent value. Nowadays this is all too well known and we are aware how these sentiments of the young can be artificially directed towards dreams of power and collective domination.

Nevertheless, this preoccupation with grandeur and with power, which is normally to be found among adolescents, does not reveal itself to a young man's consciousness in such a clear and explicit fashion; on the contrary, it remains very vague. It is only in certain cases of non-evolution or of pathological evolution that this idea of grandeur and of domination will develop on its own, sometimes till it becomes a monstrosity.

The feeling for grandeur is really the expression in an emotional form of the confirmation which a young man has received of his value and of his strength, and it takes the form of an idea of predestination. It is this unconfessed belief which makes a young man so susceptible to the influences which will be brought to play on him, for he has the sense that this is a "necessity" for him; it will also make him implacably hostile to any social order which has reserved no place for him. It is not a question of abstract ideas but of sentiments which play a real part in his life: his importance, his necessity, his destiny, a young man does not learn of these by his intelligence, he experiences them, through the impulse of his personality. He hears and responds to a call which is in some ways a nominal one. But where does this call come from? He is at an age when, almost in spite of himself, he can feel creation palpitating, he seems to be bathed in light, he collaborates as a real element of mystery in the forebodings of the evening and of the night, and when faced with the indifference of men acts as a kind of accomplice with nature in her beauty. The call comes yet again. . . . Truth, beauty, justice, duty, these words which up to then have seemed a little disturbing, for there was something dull and impersonal about them, now take their part with the choir of voices which are calling. These abstract words come to life and start to speak; they ask for everything; and because he feels that he can give them powerful assistance, assistance which will be conclusive, according to his illusion—because he believes himself to be indispensable for the preservation of beauty, of greatness, of truth, a young man will respond. He is asked for collaboration, for sacrifice, for submission, for the gift of self.

If need be he will impose them on himself.

IV

In the hierarchy of values which are capable of rousing him, justice holds the first place. It has a place ahead of the love of pure truth, ahead of beauty, *and perhaps because injustice, by showing him immediately where his activity should be exerted in order to establish an order in conformity with his still somewhat exaggeratedly simple ideals, it becomes the most evident personification of evil; it will thus be often enough as a mark of resentment that a young man performs his first act as a member of the community.* This is a profound error, sometimes an irreparable one, and which, by taking possession of the whole being, can become a substitute for the gift of self, and can give the illusion that it is this gift, and can prevent all later developments. To approach social life in a spirit of resentment, and as a reaction to injustice, is to run the risk of assuming that the attempt to give the world the shape which one has imagined it should have is an act of adherence and of sacrifice, and means setting out in the pursuit of a false self-centred satisfaction.

On its own side, the poetical awakening which is so often to be found in an adolescent or a young man between the ages of fifteen and eighteen years, and which is usually freely laughed at because it only leads to bad verse or to clumsy imitations, is nevertheless the expression of a moment of universal communion, a moment of really rich emotion. The duration of the sincerity of this poetic illusion is very short and it is only by means of artifices that those who believe they are destined to become voices of the world are able to retain a real relation with nature. Very often, after a few months, all that remains are a few stereotyped characteristics. This poetic movement is followed by a very marked need for synthesis, and it is the period of adherence to a philosophic synthesis, an adherence which excludes and despises agnosticism even in its more mitigated forms, and which will provide the mind with a fundamental armament, from which it will never again be parted. A social conception will often take the place of a philosophy; a denial, or to be more exact a system of philosophic denial, represents in an adult a very positive system, which responds to this need for a synthesis, even if it only leads to negative conclusions. If his intellectual formation leads to a metaphysical conception of the world, or to a refusal to ascribe to the world any significance, these two extreme formulas will be the conclusions which a young man has reached, with the full power of his sincere mind and with an unconscious pride in himself, and which he will carry away with him as a treasure of priceless value. Whatever the value of the view of the world which he will reach in his mind (or rather which his masters will make him reach, without his being aware of it) it will in fact mean for him a fortune of great value. He will never imagine that he could have given himself over to a different system, and being sure of his own opinion, will view with disdain every system except his own. It thus happens that while he will tend to despise a conception of life which differs from his own, he will also tend to despise social conceptions, rationalities, and religions which differ from his own. Educators, unfortunately, all too often believe that this contemptuous stage is the beginning of solid convictions and are unaware that if the evolution becomes fixed in a contempt for all that is not "oneself," then this is only the sign that there has been a hold-up, a lack of enrichment, a veiling of thought.

The magnificent expansion of sympathy which an adolescent had felt for all forms of life, ends all too often, owing to an educational deviation, in disdain and contempt; it would seem that this does not correspond to the Catholic ideal in the profound sense of the word.

A philosophical system, which is the product of adult syntheses, can thus be quite a source of danger for an adolescent, who himself lacks the elements which went to make up the synthesis, and is fascinated by the special magical quality which words hold for him at that age. The programme, fortunately, takes into account, and progressively becomes more concerned with positive studies, the natural and other sciences, thus forcing him to return to the concrete.

The acceptance of the concrete, of detail, for which too many of our masters showed contempt when teaching us, at a time when we were all too ready to despise them, is the normal stage at which the period of syntheses and *a priori* convictions should reach its completion: the acceptance of having to submit to reality, of beginning serious study, of freeing oneself from adolescence. Having loved flowers, then to start studying botany; having "understood" the world by means of the affections, to try and understand a small fraction of it intellectually; the acceptance of methods which at first seem to be forbidding, of disappointments, of fresh starts; travelling by roads which are without beauty. New and partial syntheses will only be formed considerably later, when truth, beauty and justice will assume another meaning, having in them more that is human and belongs to the past, and becoming more worthy of love and admiration. But these are the joys of a man which are not even imagined at the age of twenty years.

The acceptance of the principle of reality entails something else as well; this is the acceptance of the surroundings in which we live, the acceptance of the nation to which we belong, of the civilization surrounding us, of the religion in which we have been brought up. It is true that in many cases this acceptance is deferred or even refused; this may be for very noble or for very base motives. An adolescent, when freed from the all-powerful influence of his family, finds himself faced with an alarming solitude, and without owning to it, needs approval just as much as a child, needs something which will replace the absolute authority of his father, in fact needs a master. Of course, he wishes to have chosen this master freely for himself, but in return he expects, from the one to whom he will give his affection, that he will receive a similar affection, one that is both worthy and virile. What a small number of young people, at that moment of solitude in their lives, receive the least mark of attention from some man whom they admire and would gladly choose as an adviser, and who should be aware of the admiration of which he is the object? How many men would have become better if only other men had not just let them pass by as if they were mere numbers, without really seeing them, without understanding them, without having made use of some word or action which would have aroused in them a virile acceptance of life, before they started looking for the answer to their questions in the newspaper-stall at some station. . . . There are political systems which rely entirely on the need which a young man feels for a "duce."

It is all too often forgotten that men think when faced with themselves, they are constantly reducing their personal futures to a system, as Blondel would say, and cannot live facing a void. The fact of entering a society, of being welcomed by it, of finding in it that which will add to one's development, is not a sort of falling away, an absorption, a destruction of the true self, as some supporters of doctrine of "the will to power" would have it, but is in fact a happy event, one which is to be expected and is healthy, for it gives the new personality an assurance and an aim; it gives form to the desires, gives a definite direction to those diverse and over-vague possibilities which rise up from the depths of the adolescent soul. Apart from quite exceptional cases, the man who does not give himself, whether he refuses to sacrifice one of his possibilities of development, or else intends to keep his individuality to himself and to live apart from society, usually from that moment ceases to develop, and spends a good part of his life trying to make himself equal with the rest of the world, or simply in trying to find a way of life or a profession that will suit him.

An adolescent is thus looking for a positive work to do. He is groping his way in order to find that environment which will correspond with his aspirations, while at the same time he is thinking how he can mould his immediate surroundings to him according to his way of seeing things, according to his sense of order. In all organized societies these needs of the adolescent are taken into account, needs both of his own life and of his family, so that he may find his place, may give himself, and may become part of a broader environment. It was at the time when puberty was drawing to its close, round about the age of eighteen years, an age when the main outlines of his world should have been completed, when the personality of a young man was in a framework within which it could develop, and already had within it the as yet incomplete capabilities of a man, that the famous Athenian oath, one of the finest flowersof the eternal soul, was taken. It was on the average about the age of seventeen years that a young Roman, knowing what he was doing and already having enough resources of his own, used to enter civil life. This public acceptance of a young man into the social family is not a special acquirement of civilization, and it would seem that in later times at least, less and less importance has been ascribed to this gesture by which a young man gives himself to his environment, except perhaps in English society. The totalitarian states have on the other hand returned to the primitive rites, and this outlook should be condemned *a priori*. Among the peoples of Australasia and Polynesia, for instance, as soon as the beard starts to grow, the adolescents are placed apart and instructed in moral rules, in customs, in sacred legends, which a man should know, defend and love. They are subjected to certain moral trials and certain physical sufferings, and when circumcision is performed at that time, it has to be borne along with certain other pains (such as tearing away a strip of skin) without the least sign of weakness, at the risk of being put to death or being placed among the women and children. In such a case, the initiation into the life of the tribe is accompanied by a kind of test of virility, with a view to doing away with deficiencies, as we have shown. In short, puberty is regarded as having evolved spontaneously to the offering of the self to the tribe or the nation, and it is at the time when all the needs of a man are at last ready to take on a final form, that the ceremony of initiation brings the solution.

V

The appearance of puberty in a child breaks up the limitations of the family circle. As we have seen, the most noticeable characteristics of that age are the appearance of physical courage (and the appearance of moral courage in rough outline, which is, however, conditioned by a number of things); also the appearance of a natural capacity for governing the emotions and restraining the reflexes.

A child's acts of independence become transformed into attitudes of independence, and finally into independence itself; it begins to seek for a wider environment, more congenial to an adolescent personality; it becomes sensitive to all theories which respond to its needs, and is specially vulnerable to all visionary theorizing; it feels a great need to take part in all forms of life, a capacity for endowing the universe, whether animate or inanimate, with multiple souls, from which there is derived a tendency to religious sentimentality and all kinds of mysticism, whether good or bad.

But the phenomenon which dominates all else is the awakening of the sexual instinct.

If we have not begun with that, as is usually done, it is because the awakening of the senses, closely connected with the physiological transformations which are taking place in the young man, is only one aspect, though an essential one, of what is taking place in him, and the evolution of the type we have descried is only possible—it only rarely conforms to the ideal pattern we have described—as long as the awakening of the senses does not impede this evolution, or cause a deviation, or even hold it up altogether. The idea that the only end of puberty is to bring a young man on to the time of sexual initiation and that this should be done as rapidly and as simply as possible, seems to us an over-simplified physiological opinion, which deserves rather severe handling. An adolescent who has arrived at puberty needs advice. Faced with the organic disturbances which are taking place within him, frightened by alarming tittle-tattle, all too often he imagines he is lost, that his faculties will be destroyed, that his will can no longer obey him, since he has given way. The young man becomes afraid and is afraid with a shamefaced fear which, especially in Protestant countries or in irreligious surroundings, will make him turn to the specialists in such questions who are turning them to their own account. Stanley Hall tells how he bought, in an office of this sort, a thousand distracted letters from young men, and could have obtained a million of them in the same house. This gives some idea of the important part played by the sexual question at that period, but it is also a measure of the importance of the struggle which a young man puts up against such difficulties, and the importance of the moral factor. The most important thing at such a time is not so much that there should be no fall, which does not often happen, but that in the course of going over the authoritative principles to which an adolescent will almost certainly give his allegiance, the authoritative nature of these moral laws should continue to be recognized, and that the idea of good and evil should not become dissolved in certain vague notions of psychology. *Now, in the eyes of a number of educationalists who claim to be scientific, the problem of sexual education merely consists in keeping the question within the exclusive framework of physiological needs, and in removing it from the control of moral laws; their aim is to free the tendencies which form the psychological make-up of a young man from all control other than a care for hygiene.* If this care for hygiene comes to have a commanding position, then its importance will become exaggerated, and thus a young man's mind will easily become warped as regards the consequences of certain acts for which he may have been responsible. There is nothing to be gained by this; all that happens is that a struggle of conscience, which at least has as its consequences an improvement in moral quality, is replaced by worries of a hypochondriac kind, which are both depressing and useless, and end by the young man becoming more and more isolated through worrying about himself. Furthermore, certain confessors sometimes make the mistake of dramatizing the "hygienic" results of sexual sin. This is of no real assistance to an adolescent to get himself in hand, but merely adds to his sense of guilt, a fear of disease and of natural inferiority which may cause him no small damage. It is a young man's moral sense which must be preserved, and in order to do this it is necessary, in spite of any qualms which one may have, that it should be in an atmosphere, not of discouragement and fear, but of healthy optimism.

A certain optimism is also very reasonable when one realises how widespread the practice of self-abuse is.

This self-abuse is compensatory, in the sense that it would be greatly reduced if society interposed no barrier between the young people of different sexes. This also means that where this barrier is artificially broken, in youth movements, youth hostels, and the like, whatever their protagonists may say, the atmosphere will be essentially sexual. We know what liberty there is and the confidences which have been received from the feminine population of day-schools, of universities and even of certain "up-to-date" boarding schools, will enlighten us on this point, if there is any need for it.

Everything which is likely to compromise the work of protection is harmful. We must have the courage to stand up to certain forms of irony, to the facile contempt with which certain "emancipated" minds regard the discipline of moral principles. Human experience is there, however, to prove that only those people have developed among whom sexual morals have been the object of a genuine discipline, and apart from any question of religion, the problem has been in a sense resolved by experience. A thing which can cause disaster in a young man is the reading of some licentious book, for this may let loose in him a flood of impulses which he will have difficulty in resisting. His curiosity will urge him towards books of this kind, but at the same time an internal resistance will become formed in him and he will usually be able to overcome his unhealthy curiosity, if, in order to obtain such a work, he has to face difficulties and to feel shame keenly. The public display and sale of certain volumes or reviews bring up the same problem every day, and end by carrying away the curious. The direct consequences of such reading can be incalculable, apart from the doubt which it can arouse as to the legitimacy of moral laws (other serious works can produce the same results), by their influence on the future of the young reader. If, by this means, he is led on to a premature and frequently most unfortunate sexual initiation, he will not free himself and he may become an adolescent and *later a man whose sole emotional bond linking him with the external world is sexuality.* The only appeal of which this adolescent will from that time onwards be aware will be that of the flesh and once this appeal has been responded to without moral restraint, without reserve, the rest of the world will no longer exist. The harm done is not confined to the actual fault; *what happens is that there is no evolution outwards, towards other people, or if it does take place, then it is limited to what can give extra gratification to the pleasures of sex.*

Such a personality cannot, will never be able to escape from the egotistical stage and should it achieve communion with nature, this will only be in proportion as it can be converted symbolically into personal pleasure. Most of the sensual poets that we know of have never gone beyond this stage, and have never reached the point of giving themselves to anybody or anything. They are magnificent social monsters, but their egotism is the expression of arrested development, not of genius. All vicious people are not poets, however, and the ordinary ones among them, after the fire of straw has consumed them, are left with narrow personalities, with no capability for love or devotion, or for taking any real part in the life of the community. They have never been deeply stirred by an idea, have never paid any attention to any values which are not sensual, have never understood a genuine sacrifice, and finally have become absolutely incapable of human love, for human love, if it is to persist, needs sublimation first of all, and will only be maintained by constant sublimation.

After a young man has thus been drawn away from the environment which should almost completely absorb him, socially and morally and intellectually, this premature sensuality will finally abandon him and leave him all alone, free of all shackles and yet incapable of desire, and life will soon seem to him to be one vast desolate solitude, positively hostile, and more and more useless. Psychoanalysts have no difficulty in discovering sexual complexes in young candidates for suicide.

Self-abandonment to sensuality is thus the chief obstacle to normal evolution. At least, that is so if we admit that men can only come to flower through an altruistic participation in social and spiritual life. If, on the other hand, we hold that the ideal man should be a cold and utilitarian individualist, then premature sensuality should be cultivated as an almost infallible means to this.

In this region the influence of the parents is naturally reduced. There are fathers who wish to be by all means the friends of their sons and who give them advice. It is our opinion that a father can from time to time give excellent advice to his sons, but only rarely, and on the other hand we do not believe it is possible for a father really to be the confidential friend of his son and *vice-versa*. His rôle is to be an "example."

He certainly will be able to receive some confidences and it must be possible for the son to speak freely to him, indeed in certain cases this is of supreme importance, but he cannot hope or wish for more. Little by little, in proportion as his son's personality develops, he will notice that spontaneous and absolutely sincere reflexions become rarer; this may be a little painful to observe, but it is inevitable. No man is an open book nor can he be, not even your own child. Those who imagine the contrary are deceiving themselves badly. The same reflexions hold true for mothers who wish to go on being the friends, the confidantes, the "mummies" of their daughters. On the other hand, when her daughter reaches the age of puberty, a mother will have every chance, if she has not already done so, for explaining to her the biological phenomena which interest her, and of which she is clearly aware. We must not, however, lose sight of the fact that all this is the answer to questions which have engaged a normal child from its earliest years and the ideal solution for which is progressive initiation on the part of the mother, according to circumstances, and the age and powers of understanding of the child. Nobody is better suited than a mother to do these things.

A similar situation does not exist between a father and a son. Sexual reserve, in conversation between healthy men of different ages, is far more marked than among women. In a general way, furthermore, modesty is much less developed in the average woman than in the average man, which is no doubt according to nature, but it sets certain problems. As I see things, biological initiation in girls will be all the better for being the work of the mother and will be performed without difficulty for most of the time, whereas a boy will gain by being taught by the general teacher. It goes without saying that it would be absurd to give such a lesson in a country school, in which all the children will have found all the answers to their curiosity from the age of seven or eight years, by watching the life around them and taking part in all the activities.

But the influence of the parents can, indirectly, be enormous. Their first duty is to keep an eye on the family atmosphere, to watch over books, newspapers, conversations, parties, cinema programmes, the theatre and the wireless. Nor can they rest content with the idea that the sodality, the football club or the scouts will solve these problems, of whose existence and complexity they are fully aware, but which they find all the more annoying in that they feel they are incapable of dealing with them. Parents must never lose sight of the fact that, at the moment when this instinct awakens, their sons and daughters should be living under the best possible conditions for it to take on healthy and normal forms. If a child was kept at home from the age of twelve to eighteen years (without ever going away), and went through puberty solely among people of the same sex, it would experience certain interior movements which bore it towards certain companions whose voices, faces, bodies and minds responded to the vague desires surging up within it. It may even happen that this sexual instinct, once it has been polarized towards a homosexual being, will never become completely detached from it, or even may never become detached at all. Instinct tends to continue in the forms which it originally received.

It is thus important that in family life, in family gatherings, in normal life to be exact, special opportunities should be given for this instinct, which is seeking for objects, to polarize itself towards beings of the opposite sex. A too long existence in common of young people of the same sex, the organization of a life for youth which will usually take a child away from its family background, the only one in which its evolution can take place normally and healthily, are not only ill-omened because of the danger which they entail, but also because they prevent the normal development of those social forms which the sexual instinct should create in the soul of an adolescent.

Parents must therefore insist on undertaking the care of their children themselves, and not be content with a club or the scouts or some sporting association undertaking to educate them; they must organize their family life and take trouble about it so that it will be both pleasant and welcoming. Their big boys or their big girls are still children: birds which return to the nest in the evening . . . . Knocks will now come more frequently, it will be more difficult to keep order, but intelligent and discreet watchfulness is more necessary than ever before.

J

CHAPTER NINE

Adolescence
The Age of Anxiety

I

"When I was six years old I used to think," was said to me by a little girl of eleven years old, who lived in the neighbourhood of Louvain, but whose parents, when they moved, always went in the direction of the centre and the south-west of the country, "that beyond Tirlemont the world came to an end. Yes, beyond Tirlemont there was only a kind of hedge, and that beyond the hedge there was nothing at all. One day, you took us for a drive in your car. I had never been to Tirlemont; we passed through the town and I was looking out for the hedge. But the country went on and on, Nobody seemed to find this strange. This made a strange impression on me, but I did not dare to say anything."

I remember the drive that this little girl was talking about. It was a drive like many others. None of us who were with her had any suspicion of the important discovery that she made on that day, or of the very unusual state of soul which she went through for some hours. It was only five years later, in a chance conversation, that I learnt how this child had seen us crossing "the ends of the earth," and risking ourselves in the region beyond her real world, without showing any surprise.

Thus all the real lives of children escape us, even when they seem simple and transparent, and not only their lives, but the overthrowing of their ideas about things, of the little scaffoldings which they have built up in their minds. They re-create in proportion as they see things falling in, and each time they tell themselves that they have at last found the truth. All this takes place simply and normally, without the least appearance of weariness, without any self-distrust.

We know all that we went through on our own, the bounties we received and the frights we experienced; nothing is more ridiculous than when a teacher claims that he thoroughly knows the children in his care.

Being in charge of an adolescent is even more difficult, and we can almost all say of our own adolescence: we went through it alone, in a state of interior exaltation, in a state of doubt, agreeing with the things said by every creature and every thing, but decided against ourselves, hesitating and impulsive at the same time, incapable of passing on our dreams, our disappointments or our assurances, convinced that our lives would be longer, fuller and richer than those of other men, but yet not being really sure of our courage or our fidelity, of our capacity to realize the innumerable plans which were heaping up within us, divided between the sense of sin and the desire for holiness, unsatisfied with our physical nature which is at the same time submissive and anarchic, drawn with bitter anxiety towards everything which could give some meaning to our deep dissatisfaction and its elusive splendour, wondering to which appeal we should respond. Those who spoke to us, and gave us advice, thought we were more simple than we were, and did not understand how things really were with us. And how can we explain to anyone that we have just gone past the hedge that lies at the end of the world?

Again, most of the time we do not understand how it is and why that adolescents choose such and such a trade, grow excited over some ideology or some myth, give themselves up to some movement, submit to some ideal, or follow some vocation.

II

In spite of all the riches of adolescence, inferiority complex can play an enormous part, and that is why we propose to say a few words about it.

Nothing is more difficult to define than this complex.

There are many who imagine that it is an idea of inferiority, a sense of incapacity, the conviction that one is good at nothing, or at least, that one has not the same capacities as others of the same age. It is not that at all, but something quite different.

The inferiority complex is a combination of compensations and adaptations by means of which a human being struggles against the evidence of his inferiority in some sphere and succeeds in deluding himself and often enough other people as well.

The complex is thus founded on a sense of inferiority (real or imaginary), a refusal of the conscious mind to admit this inferiority, by a more or less conscious struggle, which can be an astonishly skilful one, against this evidence.

In this state of soul, it is not the idea of inferiority which dominates, but rather a combination of elements obstinately opposed to such an idea, bragging, stubbornness, aggressive displays, bluff, and so on. Those who are subject to this complex try to build up a façade of artificial "power," behind which inferiority can only be discovered after a very prolonged search; this discovery is sometimes impossible, if the subject is intelligent enough. We all know how those who declare they have no confidence in their own judgement cling most resolutely to their way of seeing things, while those who say that they are lacking in will-power cling most obstinately to their point of view. With such people a superficial admission of inferiority reveals that fundamentally they have immense self-confidence. We can here see from the life the phenomenon of compensation thanks to which an individual is able to live along with the idea which is discouraging him.

This way of behaving must in no sense be confused with modesty. The latter is just the moral and social way of dealing with the power complex, and by means of this it is possible to keep the balance between the two forms of pride, the positive form and also the negative, the idea of inferiority. Or, if you prefer, modesty brings to order at the same time the two complexes, that of power and that of inferiority.

Here is a typical example of inferiority complex. John did badly in mathematics but very well in French and Latin and in everything to do with literature; he found this failure in mathematics definitely humiliating. No young man will admit that a reverse may be due to some lack on his side. In order to avoid humiliation John therefore sets up a complete defence mechanism, in which, unfortunately, his parents and teachers may be all too ready to collaborate. John will then come to the conclusion, and will do so more and more, that the mathematical and literary aptitudes are definitely opposed to each other. He will decide that an aptitude for mathematics is a poor affair, suitable for second-rate minds, which are incapable of appreciating either ideals or art. (We are already coming across an attitude of contempt). Furthermore—he will go on to think—literature is the true expression of men, and he will thus decide to give himself to literature altogether, while he will turn away from mathematics with disdain. From then onwards he and literature are bound up with each other, at least so John persuades himself.

Up to now we have only been concerned with an anodyne, but the time comes to choose a career. The inferiority complex, which has developed as we have described, is going to play a predominant part in this decision. "What is wrong with this?" you may say. Certainly, if a young man who is attracted by art is able to give himself up to useful work, all is well; but if he is only a nondescript pupil, whose taste for literature has no other foundation than a reaction in defence against his failure in mathematics, it will be a good thing for him to know in time that he is only the victim of a mirage.

A contempt for some branch of the programme, a dislike of some form of activity, may often conceal a weakness, and the cause of this weakness is often not the one that is imagined. It may not be due to a real lack of aptitude for mathematics, but to a bad start in this branch of study, to bad teaching, to a reverse which has not been understood and wrongly interpreted. When faced with a failure in studies, the only sane and normal attitude for those who have failed is not to turn in upon themselves and thus to submerge themselves in the complex, but to set resolutely to work. If a pupil really lacks some gift, he will soon have the proof of this, and he will then have no cause for doubting that mathematics are not his strongpoint; there will be no question about it. But should he be able to overcome the impression he has received and the figures as well, then what a victory there will be! He will perhaps come to love what he was tempted to detest.

An inferiority complex is thus not a combination of conscious reactions to a conscious sense of inferiority. Similar reactions are often to be found, and may be useful or harmful, according to the case, but they cannot be described as complexes. That term is limited to that combination of instinctive reactions which tend to protect the subject from becoming aware of real inferiority. It is at the same time a form of defence and of compensation, and this complex is in itself *a priori* neither harmful nor beneficial. It is a psychological mechanism, a blind mechanism.

Teachers must be careful not to bring about the birth of an inferiority complex; they should instead help the child to bring to an end the complex which has begun to form.

This is relatively easy when dealing with normal children, but becomes more and more impossible when morbid factors enter in. We should perhaps only speak of inferiority complexes in pathological cases, but, according to Adler's theories, the use of the term has been expanded so as to include a considerable number of normal and ordinary cases.

Observe the attitude of a child towards its parents, towards its father especially, also its elder brothers and sisters. This attitude is a complicated one. A child chafes at the position of inferiority that it holds in regard to these people. Its behaviour is partly inspired by the desire to become their equal. There is thus a certain inferiority complex in every child, even in one which is growing up in normal conditions. The ego of the child can only assert itself fully by means of this disposition. This only becomes a bad thing if the parents and the brothers and sisters, by taking up a clumsy and provocative attitude, aggravate the child's normal and real sense of inferiority. If they are harsh towards its weakness, if they oppress it, they will end by producing in it an abnormal need for compensation, and, in consequence, reactions which may prove unfortunate.

A little boy may think that he is loved as much as his father, by all, but especially by his mother. If this child, which, just because it is a child, already has a sense of inferiority, notices that its mother shows special marks of affection for its father, then its sense of inferiority will be sharply aggravated. It is shown its nothingness, and this it cannot accept, and the more its nerves are affected, the less will it accept this. This can lead to violent reactions, hatred, contempt, unsociability, all impressions which will leave their mark on the soul for life. A child believes it is the equal of others, and its ideas have been organized in such a way as to protect this sense of equality. When it discovers this special affection which it did not suspect, this will seem to be thoroughly unjust, unjustified, and intolerable. When it has reached adolescence, the least incident will revive the complex, and give it a fresh stimulus.

As another example, let us think of a child not gifted with much intelligence. Its results at school are poor, but this child does not admit its lack of intelligence; it does not even think of it. By its application, however, by the slow building up of an attitude which has been wonderfully adapted, it exerts itself to make up for this lack, and it is often successful. There are many compensated weaklings who are rated too high by those around them.

All too often, unfortunately, the sense of insufficiency is only avoided by a contemptuous attitude for the things of the mind; indeed, a child may often refuse to study, and if an attempt is made to make it do so, it rebels. This may lead to unsociability, to its running away from home, to worse still.

Teachers must take care to help such a child to accept reality, while trying, at the same time to make this reality acceptable. The child should be encouraged, and be praised for everything it is able to do; it should be stimulated in efforts to attain compensation by work, and emphasis should be laid on the good results achieved. To treat a feeble child—or indeed any child—as if it was an idiot and an imbecile, is quite disastrous. If its results at school are bad, there is no need for anything further to show the child its insufficiency.

Parents must, however, be careful not to blame the teachers for these bad results. This would be a loop-hole of which their child would make full use; it would make out that it was the victim of antipathy, of lack of understanding, of unjust severity, of unkind hostility.

For a child, the results of its examinations at school are the normal way of getting to know itself and for comparing itself with other children. Their significance must be neither over-stressed nor under-rated; a child must just be helped to face what life requires from it.

For one who is rather weak in intellect, sport is sometimes a means of regaining his position socially. Sporting circles usually despise the things of the intellect! This attitude is often no more than a means of compensation, and in the same way those who are incompetent jeer at the specialists whom they refer to contemptuously as "technicians." In return, those with a poor physique have a contempt for sport, and specialists look with disdain on general ideas; such are the complex attitudes inspired by the struggle against the sense of inferiority. We must not look for moderation, for the golden mean, among these. Extreme attitudes, which they will alone consider as virile and straightforward, do no more than conceal a wrong mental adaptation to life.

This disdain for physical effort or for the work of the mind are points of view which can be full of consequences, for such an attitude prevents any contact between the despiser and the despised, and it above all prevents the one who despises from filling up the gap from which he suffers.

To sum up, any inferiority complex which tends to make up for a real lack by an artificial attitude is bound to have thoroughly bad results; it will either lead to "escape" or else to savage and perhaps revolutionary behaviour.

Most complexes appear about the age of five years. By the ages of ten or twelve years they are clearly formed, and usually they get steadily stronger. Most of them, fortunately, play a useful part in the evolution of the mind.

At the time of puberty or shortly afterwards, parents begin with rather a shock to see the reality concealed beneath the outward appearance of their child. They are astonished at finding that the difference is so great between what a child is in reality and what they imagine it to be, between what it is and the idea that they had of it, between what they thought it was and all that it lacks . . . . they then try to adjust themselves . . . . but how is this to be done? Must the little creature be humiliated, and made to feel something of reality on the raw? This may sometimes succeed, if the child is intelligent and loyal, but it is to be feared that from then onwards this child may lose confidence in itself. Outwardly it will seem to behave as it did previously, but in its heart it will have the hidden wound of doubt and sometimes of despair, which can seldom be cured. If it is normal, well understood and advised, it may succeed in overcoming itself, in assuring itself that it really is of value, in regaining self-confidence . . . . but it may be the prey of those treatises which teach "efficiency," "the formation of the will," "world conquest," all those lamentable books which do no more than prolong illusions.

A young man, who has often been for a long time the prisoner of points of view which he has held for a long time, may have become unaffected by any form of reproach. If his parents go on obstinately, he will be found to separate himself from them more and more, taking a dislike to them, becoming indifferent, even hating them. He escapes through contempt, all the more so because at that age certain successes with girls may help to maintain his illusion of superiority.

Along with this contempt for his parents there will grow a contempt for everything his parents stand for : authority, morality, religion, their country. It is therefore all the more necessary that the fresh education of this young man should be confided to some experienced person who possesses human qualities of the highest kind. If left to himself, the young man will find his escape in the endless fields of false compensations. He must be reconquered and his affection must be won. In any case, to wish to keep a young man in an attitude of conscious inferiority would be the surest way of making him break away. There are certain young men who are nearly always in a nervous condition—not always, however—who do not always recover from these humiliations, and suffer a definite loss in their efficiency and their personalities.

In particular, as far as it is possible, a young man, who is faced with difficulties in the matter of chastity, must be prevented from asking himself the question: Am I like other people or not? There are few young people, there are even few invalids who will admit that they are inferior to others. They will drag themselves along for quite a while in a state of anxiety and they may even solve their problem by the loss of the Faith.

The complex which they will end by forming will often consist of an external hyper-purity, which is sincere and intended to defend the approaches of the soul, but which is also intended to compensate externally for the shame that is sensed within. This will separate a young man from normal contacts with reality—normal human contacts—and he will become isolated in an unyielding attitude; this will deprive him of frank relations with his fellow-creatures, and will deform his whole view of the world and of civilization.

It is impossible to avoid every difficulty, but this defence organization can often be skilfully directed and brought back to truer proportions. This is for directors of conscience to do, but will also depend on the family atmosphere.

Physical ugliness or beauty sometimes play a considerable rôle in the development of a personality. If anyone is really ugly, it is desirable that he should learn it as late as possible, and his parents should take care that he does not notice it, or the child may compensate itself for its sense of inferiority by cracking up its ugliness, turning it into a savage form of self-assertion, perhaps even going so far as to bring its moral character into conformity with it. It may even construct for itself, in some secret corner of its consciousness, a lofty idea of its intellectual and moral superiority. But, if it should prove impossible to keep up this idea of superiority, may this not lead to catastrophe, to revolt and to despair? There are those, however, who at the cost of heroic efforts are able to achieve this superiority, which should remind us that an inferiority complex does not necessarily have bad effects. Its effects are bad only when it provokes inhuman or anti-social attitudes as a means of compensation.

III

In the world of science, as in the world of intelligence, we can in the course of a few years become conversant with all that humanity has produced in the past, and we can then set out from where the current of progress has led us. It is not, however, the same in the world of the affections and morality; each one of us starts at zero and must by his own efforts renew that moral experience which all men have had to find for themselves before him. We have to discover this experience in another setting, no doubt in another atmosphere, maybe in better conditions, but none-the-less we have to go through the complete cycle, starting with our first tempers as a newborn child.

Collectively we possess, along with tradition, a moral patrimony, but this moral patrimony should not be used as if it was the rule of three: we must adapt and conform ourselves to it, and as we go along we must learn that all this has its own special difficulties. Towards the end of our lives we shall no doubt come to understand that the moral laws must be as they are and that in the long run they alone are wise. The normal reaction of a young man is not, however, to submit to the existing order, which calls for so much renunciation and offers so little immediate satisfaction. He hopes that there may be other formulas in existence, which will enable him to attain an earlier and easier equilibrium.

What he is most shocked by is that he has to grow accustomed to tolerating a certain amount of injustice, and a certain amount of disorder; he sees that, if he wishes to become the equal of preceding generations, (he becomes aware of this fairly rapidly), he must undertake a new and formidable intellectual effort. Before he accepts all this, a young man will try to recreate a world according to his own ideas, a world in which he will be immediately able to take the first place, an anti-intellectualist world.

We know the fervour with which an adolescent will seize hold of such a theory. It is not a question of special tastes but of special needs.

If a child, from the time of its first intellectual perceptions, begins to class beings and things into two categories, this is not because its mind is of a classifying type, but because things and events can only have two meanings for it; they are good or bad according to the relation which they have with its own system of thought or interests. This spontaneous classifying, (which family environment may have been training for some time past) is thus purely egocentric. A young bourgeois will judge men's behaviour quite differently from a young socialist, and in each case the judgment will be so closely bound up with the inner being of those who judge that it will seem to have an absolute and definitive value.

This classification does not come into being through an intellectual activity, but owing to the fact that the child and then the young man *take up an attitude towards the objects of their judgment.* These attitudes are usually rigid and over-simplified, (usually profoundly unjust owing to their very need for short-view justice), and the family atmosphere may either strengthen or weaken them. The same will hold true both of the schoolmaster and the university teacher.

It is in this sense that we must understand the importance of a family spirit passing from one generation to another and giving all thought and all activity a certain way of reacting: we find old families which may be liberal or conservative, diplomatic, industrial or artistic, even anarchistic. Even if a child becomes aware that it is "in chains," it is rare that it does not, along with François Mauriac, return to the road of tradition.

Everything which is likely to convince an adolescent that it is essential to overthrow the established order and to replace it by something which is more simple and more just, something which is freed from useless restraints and brings the emotional life of a man into prominence, will be welcomed.

Racialism, exaggerated nationalism, humanitarianism centred on resentment rather than love of one's neighbour, a somewhat pagan philosophy, a gospel of force, a doctrine which is as anti-intellectual as possible, thus giving priority to all the instinctive powers of self-assertion, domination and supremacy, these things of which an adolescent bears the uneasiness all at the same time, will prove favourite doctrines to which the vast mass of adolescents readily surrender. If in certain countries there is a kind of communion of youth in racial and national ideals, which are both savage and dynamic, this is not because these young people are superior to other young people, it is solely because they have been given ideals which are within their grasp, because they have been promised the world which unconsciously they desire, because this satisfies certain of their elementary aspirations.

And yet, adolescence must be left behind; what will happen to these generations when they perceive the decay, the childishness of their illusions, when, on the battlefields which from now on seem to have become inevitable, they meet the generations of those who have not too easily believed they were immortal and invincible, and whose uneasiness has had time to take on a defensive form? For uneasiness, which is the sister of self-distrust, the source of all research and of all intellectual and moral evolution, cannot be destroyed in an adolescent without running the risk of drying up at the source a whole part of the spiritual riches of men.

We certainly cannot work out all these questions, but we can understand without difficulty what riches, what a moral fortune, what discipline and what mental fertility the Graeco-Latin humanities can bring to an adolescent, when drunk in at that age of internal storms, of strange fancies, of vague and confused attempts to find easy and retrogressive forms of life.

On a mind which tends to confine itself within its own self-satisfaction and a sterilizing narcissism, they suddenly impose the grand outline of all the life of the mind since the beginning of time, they force the intelligence to suspend its judgments, they transform what seem to be absolute and urgent problems into relative and secondary questions, they give the reason the power partly to free itself from its egocentric ways. This counts for a lot.

The finest present which parents can give their children, is to confer on them, as set forth in the ancient humanities, all that nobility and greatness of soul, which are necessary in order to understand Christianity.

★   ★   ★

And then the day will come when the child will leave home; if the family atmosphere has been as it should be, then we may have confidence in his destiny, even if at the start he does not seem to take the road that we should wish.

The soul of a man will be gradually formed within him, and by increasingly concentric circles he will be drawn back to the ways of his childhood. For a long time he will remain unconscious of the love of which he was the object. It is only at the hour when he, in his turn, will hold a fragile newly-born child in his arms, that he will understand, with tears in his eyes, what you have been to him.

CHAPTER TEN

Adolescence
The Age of Subordination
The Age of Death

I

The adolescent described by M. Debesse in his book *La Crise d'Originalité Juvenile* (the crisis of youthful originality) scarcely exists. Not that we never meet with him, but when we do so we are astonished, surprised, frightened at his lack of resistance, at his docility, at the ease with which he repeats formulas which may almost certainly lead to his destruction, gaily composing his own epitaph. The most solid among these young men are not, to speak the truth, the ones who keep diaries, thus depicting and analysing themselves. These diaries give an effect of narcissism, with which only a small proportion of young people are imbued; introspection can easily become allied with a form of egotism which is of no social value, but this period of egotism, of self-analysis, of originality, of self-assertion, which only shows itself in words amongst a few, coincides with one of the first adult manifestations of the instinctive life, which is more or less to be found among all the privileged people of this life, students, children of the well-to-do classes, who have a certain amount of time at their disposal, with a vocabulary and elements of culture which help them to become aware of all that is taking place. It is also to be found among others, but then the phenomena are drowned in a collection of premature efforts to adapt themselves to daily life.

This expansion of sympathetic instincts, which is the most comprehensive form of love and which has in it the seeds of friendship, of love, of parental love, for some weeks, some days, some hours, sometimes some minutes, will illuminate the soul of the adolescent, and will reveal to him, in a total intuition, this world of values. This illumination is produced by the affective and emotional reaction of the young man when faced with some special stimulus, though the latter may have only a distant connection with any living being. It may be a sunset, a landscape, a human voice heard in the evening; a religious service, the majesty of a storm, the charm of an early morning, or some pure form, which will cause him to experience suddenly and by surprise a sense of agitation by which he is overcome; this takes possession of all his powers of defence and his reflexes, and gives this stimulus such a value that, from then onwards, everything will be sacrificed to the rediscovery of such a state. Beauty, life and truth are bound up with this experience and in certain cases, with young people who are gifted, this stimulus can be so intense that their reaction of adoration can be let loose without there being any object for it, as if the Absolute had suddenly been revealed to their souls. Many young people have thus known what they call a contact with God and have subordinated the rest of their lives to such a unique moment, to this absolute value, which has about it something that is not unlike hallucination.

May we here give a quotation from a letter to François, a schoolboy, in the little book *Culture et Education Physique* (Physical Culture and Education):

"Do you not remember, dear poet, the day when you heard that voice? I remember, you were scarcely fourteen years old. You had just come back for the Easter holidays. You had left your college on a foggy Holy Saturday in mid-April. It was cold. There were some buds which had begun to swell out on the boughs of the old alley of lime-trees, but they had not yet been noticed. You had left all that as things whose fate it is to be left behind at regular intervals and which have no right to any share in your life, and then, three weeks later, on the Sunday evening when you went back, when, in a rather morose mood, having arranged everything in your cubicle, you went down into the quadrangle to see if your friends had arrived yet, something made a profound impression on you. The lime-tree alley was waiting for you, resplendent with its young leaves, and the low rays of the setting sun produced an effect of mystery. From that day onwards you knew that you could no longer keep apart from creation. You remained silent for a long time; you found yourself beset with a sense of solemnity. In the secrecy of your soul you knew that you were part of the universe, and that it was awaiting your testimony and collaboration. The creation of the world has existed for you from that day. In the days before that twilight you did know that there is a beauty in living beings, that you could go to meet the light, that there is a pulsating life in the earth and in the heavens, a secret order which you could not discover without at the same time discovering that you were part of it. It was on that evening that you first felt within yourself an imperious need to create, to create by mingling yourself with this life, by taking your place firmly in this movement and this immensity. It was on that evening that you first had some idea of that strange thirst which was soon to make you take the world in your grasp.

You knew that you could not be mistaken about this inspiration and, without formulating it, you made a fervent vow that you would always answer: I am here. Though there was no witness to your undertaking, and no note was made of it, you know that you will have to fulfil it. You cannot renounce it without feeling you have perjured yourself, without a secret sense of degradation. From then onwards you have been linked up with the destiny of men."

II

It is in the course of these privileged moments that a man will set out in a definite direction, towards some vocation or other, or will take up some special attitude, for something genuine has happened, hard though it may be to define. Though a young man may have been but little prepared for them morally, from now on he knows that genuineness and truth exist, and he knows that he has the power of recognizing them. It may be that for the rest of his life he will never find such fullness again, but if he seeks for it, if he keeps it as the vital test, then he will receive its impress and be blessed by it. There is a whole centre of his being which he will keep alive, holding it out with his arm, above the mud of the Styx. The few men out of whom the spiritual genius of the human race has been made are those who have remained faithful to the sign of the genuine, at that absolute moment which life has given to each one of us, even if it was only a flash at the time of puberty.

If we observe this carefully we shall see that they have all refused to forget what has taken place, and that they have, within definite limits, submitted to a value. A man who speaks of values only does so sincerely if, when he does so, he is conscious of a certain attitude, of a certain tension, of a certain hour in his youth which remains illuminated somewhere within his soul and which he will always refuse to cover up, and in consequence he will always be able, when he speaks of it, to give a little sign about which there can be no mistake and which no literature can describe. You may read through ten volumes of artistic criticism without coming across one point of view which made it worth while or revealed anything like a priestly attitude towards life, but you cannot read twenty lines of Rodin without finding yourself faced with the true submission.

It would seem that the chief event of adolescence is this revelation made to the soul that there is the possibility of a universal communion, which is not always exactly recognized as the prelude to the communion of love, an event thanks to which the subject does not only take his place and find his affections settled in a certain place in the world, but he also adopts a point of view, if he is worthy of it, becomes different from everyone else, becomes a person, and can escape from the gloom of the collective destiny, by following his interior light.

This, however, remains dependent on subjects which are more or less exceptional, and can in certain circumstances be confounded with the tragic obscurity of illness; that is to say, a morbid lack of power to evolve frequently takes place, a pathological fixation at a certain stage or even a regression towards a previous stage which appears to be similar, may often be found at the same time on the road of courage and of personality. The case of a Rimbaud may savagely find its way into the series.

III

The picture which we have just been studying may in certain cases only exist in a negative form; *in fact, knowledge through sympathy is only possible if there is an accompanying restraint of the defence functions by the will.* One of these two aspects may dominate the mental processes. An adolescent may be sensitive to the values which are revealed to him by sympathy, even to the point of giving way without putting up any defence, or of giving himself for the sake of giving, taking pleasure in a certain atmosphere of suicide or of death, or more simply still, in an adventure of action for action's sake. In proportion as psychological knowledge becomes more definite do we become more aware of the extraordinary ways in which these dispositions of young people can be used. Military formations which in the end are bound to lead to suicide, as were organized among the Japanese, use being made of the Japanese tendency to self-abandonment, were, after all, no more than an extreme development of the military theories and exercises of the West. Experience has proved that the general attitude of adolescents towards death are more easy to exploit than their experience of the absolute, and that it is possible really to rely on those periods of unconcerned detachment in adolescents with regard to their education, even with a view to some particular vocation.

This tendency is very significant; it prepares an adolescent for the part which he will play in life and makes it easier for him to undertake it;

we should avoid the idea that to make use of this tendency to a considerable extent, necessarily deserves condemnation. It is, however, a good thing to know that this self-abandonment, which contains many dangers for the personality, and during which period a young man should be protected rather than exploited, can have different names: generosity, the gift of self, renunciation, pledging oneself, can be used, if so interpreted, for doubtful ends under misleading forms, such as "remaking a new world," "passing on the torch to the rising generation," and other hollow formulas, which are all the more capable of being accepted unanimously in that they are all more or less alike.

The technique of preparation for military suicide, which has been described in a number of journals, shows the effect by playing on the mind with techniques of a semi-religious and mystical type; anyone who claims that this is a matter of moral values is an impostor. Such a man should know perfectly well that it is in fact a technique for obtaining the spontaneous or anyway the freely bestowed offering of lives, and that if the young man who allows himself to be led in this way has fine moral qualities, then his exploiter is all the more vile for having made use of him for these ends, when, being himself more than ten years old, he would have been able to estimate their folly and their falsehood. It is this collective and organized lying about death which gives war its inhuman character and provides its hecatombs.

However it may be, as the result of this momentary indifference in regard to his own life, an indifference which is no more than the effect of the calling off of his defences, and not a real capacity to endure death, a young man may be led as long as the bait is given an appearance to correspond with his need of an absolute and of a synthesis, towards every facile racial, humanitarian, conservative or revolutionary ideology; every historical or geographical idea can have its martyrs, especially its soldiers, and a young man, as long as he is living thus unprotected, even feels an inclination to be satisfied with blind obedience, with unconditional enlistment.

The mysticism which is able to keep men in this state of mind of voluntary death or in lack of self-concern after adolescence, thus produces strong men, since they never seek to protect themselves, but are content to live and to act as if they might die at any moment. And indeed such men are formidable; we say formidable because they are seldom to be met with except among criminals and gangsters. Other men, even if they have enlisted under the banner of disregard for self, regain possession of themselves. Even a religious sets out to reconquer his personality, he finds once more the possibility of self-defence, becomes reasonable, active and sometimes tepid. From time to time a man stays firm till the end of his life, remains truly faithful to his early undertaking, and continues to give himself without limit. He then takes on the stature of a saint. In that case the early consent to death is gradually sublimated into an oblation, into a conscious and voluntary acceptance.

The emotional pledge undertaken at puberty has two highly different aspects. One is a positive pledge, and is the direct effect of the revelation of values by direct participation in life; the other is a passive pledge which is made because of the absence of defences. It is this second pledge which would seem to be easiest to exploit and those who remain faithful to it can only remain faithful to an early orientation, to a social attitude, which is not enlightened from within.

IV

Puberty is, however, for the greatest number, in reality the age of death; this is because the conditions of life of the greatest number do not allow them to take their bearings in such a free way. Most young people are caught at an early age in a network which compels them to be objective and reasonable and to reduce to a minimum the part which they leave to life, to a flowering without effort. They then find, especially in communities with a highly organized social life, a collection of bodies already in existence, which influence and control them so much that it is impossible or at least difficult for them to undergo such an experience. In any case this is rarely a fact which seems worthy of notice. Their need of synthesis reveals itself in a desire for realism and the denial of their own personalities will coincide with a rejection of the ultimate mysteries and problems. In the world of believers, the passive acceptance of a mass of beliefs, corresponds with this mentality; there is no great difference, from the psychological point of view, between dismissing a problem, and dismissing all facing of a solution which has been accepted wholesale. In various ways these people will develop in a state of conformity, under different names. The only regrets they will feel, as they grow old, is that they were not more completely selfish at an earlier age, that they did not get more out of life, in other words that they made too many voluntary sacrifices for the sake of values. For many men life comes to an end at puberty; their history ends before it begins.

At the present time we hear of nothing but propaganda, of methods for attracting and for holding people, how ceremonies are to be modernised and souls are to be brought back. This is no doubt absolutely necessary, but the work will be in vain if, in a society of this kind, those who have remained alive have to obey the commands of those who are dead.

It would be too simple, at the point which we have reached, to lay the blame on mankind, on the products of a certain social order, and to accuse them. A leading class has been in existence for a long time, there have been schools and universities, while education has become more or less compulsory all over the place, but in spite of that, the generations become one after the other immersed in the same murderous wars, in the same devastating idiocy, in the same abandonment of true values. But, are they being properly taught? The formation of men is far more difficult than is supposed by those who imagine they are forming them, for it is not merely a question of forming free men, a phrase which has very little meaning, but of forming men who cannot be reduced to slavery without their being aware of it.

We should, however, continue to believe. As long as an adolescent goes through this unique moment of emotional blending with things, of universal communion, as long as it is granted him to have a real contact with what is authentic and absolute, so will a sense of Beauty and Truth be preserved among men; a large number will have lived secretly in their service, and a certain number will have died without having lost the hope that they will find them again once more.